SCOTS SAWS

From the folk-wisdom of Scotland

David Murison

JAMES THIN

1981

THE MERCAT PRESS, EDINBURGH

© David Murison 1981

ISBN 0 901824 65 8

Set printed and bound in Great Britain
by Billing and Sons Limited,
Guildford, London, Oxford, Worcester.

Scots Saws

Most people know in a vague sort of way what a proverb is, though fussy pedants might easily pick holes in any compendious definition that one could offer of the word. As this book is not directed to such, we shall try to make do with a rough attempt: "a short, concise phrase or sentence in popular currency to express a general truth or a moral precept, or simply a piece of worldly wisdom". Some distinguish proverbs, which are in an unaltering set formula, as "Speak o the deil and he'll appear", "Weel begun is half dune", "Never say die", "Monie hands maks licht wark", from proverbial phrases, which can be altered or rephrased to suit the particular context, change of pronouns, he, she, they, etc., tense, mood, and the like; so "Kythe (appear) in your ain colours", as a moral exhortation, may become "He'll kythe in his ain colours yet", as a prophetic and dire warning; similarly, "To hae a ravelled pirn (bobbin) to redd, to wind a bonnie pirn, etc.", all based on the notion of a tangled bobbin and connoting an impasse or predicament. This incidentally explains the difficulty of alphabetising proverbs when so many of them may fluctuate in their initial word. There are many synonyms like aphorism, adage, maxim, truism, with subtle distinctions which will not concern us—indeed probably the old word 'saw', a saying, is as good as any for our purpose, as some of our material will extend beyond the strict limits of the proverb proper.

1

Scots Saws

At least there are certain features which recur in most proverbs, for a proverb is essentially a social phenomenon, a part of the oral tradition of a community like its ballads, folk-tales, fables, nursery rhymes, local legends and so on, handed down by word of mouth from one generation to the next; the business of a proverb is to inculcate the wisdom which the community has learned from its communal living over the centuries; they form a folk-philosophy of truisms which are a substitute among the unsophisticated for metaphysical argument. William Motherwell in his perceptive introduction to Henderson's *Scottish Proverbs* of 1832 aptly contrasts the attitude of Don Quixote, his head turned with the conventions from the text-books of courtly romance, with Sancho Panza and the down-to-earth realism and pragmatism of his proverbs. A repertoire of proverbs embodies the group morality of a somewhat worldly sort based on the main idea of making life's journey with the maximum avoidance of trouble, and of keeping going without running imprudent risks; the strongest suit is caution, restraint, moderation, and the middle path in all one's activities. The Greeks as usual had a word for it, μηδὲν ἄγαν, nothing in excess; the Romans said *"ne nimium"* and, with similar force, *"festina lente"*, hasten slowly, just as "ca cannie" is the motto of the stereotype Scot. Variants on the same theme are "Jouk (duck) and lat the jaw (wave) gae by", "Flie laich (low) and flie lang", "Aa owers (excesses) are ill", "Keep a mids (moderation) in aathing", which is practically a translation of Ovid's *"medio tutissimus ibis"*.

Hence arrogance and overweening self-confidence are to be avoided, from the notion that one must not tempt the gods or chance one's luck too far; and here again, as *hybris*, it forms the theme of early Greek drama. The higher you rise in the world, the more chance of overbalancing, and as early as the 15th century we find one of the earliest of our Scottish proverbs on this theme applied by the poet Robert Henryson in his fable of the Wolf and the Wedder, "Hall binks ar richt slidder", i.e. the seats in the houses of the great are very slippery. Pride indeed goes before a fall, and there is a saying, "He fell in the midden glowerin at the mune", which sounds like the climax of a folk-take about someone who let his fantasies outstrip his common prudence, similar to a story told about the earliest Greek philosopher, Thales.

The need for us all to be kept in our proper stations, whether through the social system and blue blood or the wage structure and the differentials, has always been a prime concern of the community and consequently of the proverb. We are told that despite the old clan- and blood-brotherhood "As Stewarts are no sib(related) to the King", and it is impertinence to make claims on the strength of the name. Even within the family there are class distinctions; "He is but Jock the Laird's brither" shows the feudal importance of primogeniture. As James Kelly, one of our early 18th-century proverb collectors, puts it, "The Scottish lairds' concern and zeal for the standing and continuance of their families makes the provision for their younger sons very small".

Another and greater risk in life is marriage, and as the advice of *Punch* is followed by only a small minority, avoidance is not the subject of many proverbs, but there are plenty to tell the rustic moralist, once he is in the net, how to make the best of it and what signs of discord and trouble to look out for. Proverbs on women, wives, and marriage are legion, most of them of a rather cynical and misogynistic cast, and presumably the creation of the male chauvinist pig in the domineering wife and mother-in-law tradition, and Scotland has its share: "Ye may drive the deil into a wife but ye'll ne'er ding (beat) him oot o her", "Better half-hangit than ill-mairriet", "An ill wife and a new-kindilt candle suld hae their heids hauden (held) doun", "He has faut (need) o a wife that mairries mam's pet", "Aa are guid lasses, but whaur do the ill wives come frae?", which is to say with Kelly; "Nobody can blame young women from putting their best side outmost and concealing their bad humours till they get husbands".

The third great hazard is extravagance and debt. To avoid want you must not waste, even taking it to extremes in "Better belly rive (burst) than guid meat spill (spoil)", and thrift and frugality are the way to weather the rainy day which must inevitably come to us sooner or later; "Aye keep something for a sair leg", "He that spends his gear afore he gets it, will hae little guid o't". No doubt it is from such maxims that the Scots have got their reputation for parsimony. But they are in fact the characteristic of the peasant mentality everywhere, born of real need and indigence. And it may be noted that thriftiness and greed are carefully distinguished in our proverbs; while one is warmly commended, its excess is always disapproved of, and the miser is held up to ridicule. "Ye wad mairry a midden for the muck", "Ye hae a crap for aa corn", and to intensify the degree of acquisitiveness some add "and a baggie for rye"; similarly, "The deil's greedy but ye're misleared (avaricious)". There is also the practical consideration that parsimony may overreach itself and spoil the ship for a pennyworth of tar as the saying is, or, in its Scots equivalent, "Mony ane tines the half-merk whinger (dagger) for the hapenny whang (strap)". In general "it's guid to be sib to siller", and "It's no tint that a friend gets" is an admonition to mingle friendship and generosity with self-interest.

In matters of speed too, the golden mean is urged between the two extremes of precipitateness and sloth, in the vein of "more haste, less speed"; "Hastie was hanged", we are told, "but Speed o fit wan awa (escaped)", i.e. it is safer to be wary than rash, and in *The Cherrie and the Slae*, the moral allegory by the 16th century Scottish poet Alexander Montgomerie (and a mine of proverbial sayings and aphorisms) we read, "Untimeous spurring spills the steed". There is however one exception, "Naething suld be dune in haste but grippin o fleas", which saving phrase was no doubt added by some rustic humorist from personal experience. Both sayings incidentally have Italian equivalents.

Proverbs of course can be contradictory, according as circumstances alter and the speaker's point of view varies. So we are told on the one hand that "Absence makes the heart grow fonder" and on the other "Out of sight, out of mind". You pay your money and you take your choice, because popular wisdom is invariably empirical, pragmatic, and opportunist, like that of the man whose advice to his son was, "Honesty's the best policy—I've tried baith"; while we have the converse in "Lang leal (honest), lang puir".

Industry and productivity are always commended as conducive to comfort: "A workin hand is worth a gowpin (two handfuls) o gowd", "A gangin fit is aye gettin", and the idle are to be associated with the devil, who can always find some work for them. Again this stems from the realities of the subsistence economies of mediaeval Europe, where failure to labour the earth properly could mean actual starvation. But some cynic in more affluent times added to the last the postscript, "though it be but a thorn or a broken tae", as a side-swipe at those whose desire to "get" becomes obsessive.

The devil himself was treated by the Scots with a certain humorous tolerance, so long as they believed that he had backed the wrong horse and was bound to fail in the end. Now they don't seem to be so sure and treat his philosophy with some circumspection, as they used to do in the days when they popularly called him the "Guidman" and dedicated a piece of land, "the deil's croft or fauld", to him, just to keep in his good graces. Despite the teaching and preaching of the Kirk, the common people have always shown a certain ambivalence in their attitude to good and evil, with a hankering to worship luck, and have fluctuated throughout their history between faith and superstition. Indeed we are told that "The deil's aye guid to his ain", that he's "no waur than he's caed"; that he "bides his day", which must go back to the practice of witchcraft when the witch who gave herself over to the devil had a day appointed when he would come to claim her, as he did with Faust and Don Juan.

There is of course hardly any aspect of the human condition or any activity—physical, mental, or moral—in human life for which there is no saying, apophthegm or the like. Andrew Henderson in his collection of Scottish proverbs of 1832 distributed half of his 3000-odd proverbs, not all of them exclusively Scottish, under about 130 categories, but finally gave up the attempt and slumped the other half under Truisms and Miscellaneous. Among these are anger: "He sud be seindle (seldom) angry that has few to mese (appease) him"; beauty: "A bonnie bride's sune buskit"; caution: "Ne'er put out your hand farer than your sleeve will reach"; courage: "Naething sae crouse (jaunty) as a new-washen louse", though the application is somewhat ironical, and we might add the common exhortation, "Set a stout hert to a stey (steep) brae"; dirt, which is proverbially lucky, is commended with us too in one of the pithiest and tersest of our proverbs, "The clartier the cosier", and that rather odd novel of Miss Elizabeth Hamilton,

The Cottagers of Glenburnie, written in 1808 as a manifesto for cleanliness and hygiene, is full of sayings of slatternly complacency; early rising: "They that get the word (reputation) o sune risin may lie in their bed aa day", and why shouldn't they, for "They that are early up and hae nae business, hae either an ill bed, an ill wife, or an ill conscience".

Economy, as we have seen, is constantly urged, even in diet, "Lay your wame to your winnin", i.e. match your appetite with your income; forbearance and mutual tolerance are implied in "Let a be for let a be"; friendship inspires some shrewdly cynical caution, "A friend to ane is a friend to nane", which goes back to Aristotle, "Nae friend like the penny", "Try your friend ere ye need him", "If a man's gaun doun the brae, ilk ane gies him a jundie (jostle)". On health most countries agree on the common-sense essentials like avoiding cold or wet feet: "Better wear shune than sheets" is a Scots way of putting it.

Human life may be illustrated by the truism, "The langer we live, we see the mae ferlies (the more wonders)"; there is a palpable hit on suspicion and jealousy in "If the auld wife hadna been in the oven hersel, she ne'er wad hae thocht o luikin for her dochter there"; on kindness there is again some canny equivocation, "A man may be kind and gie little o his gear", but "Kindness comes o will; it canna be coft (bought)"; in the matter of kissing, young ladies are provided with *le mot juste* when the salutation is unwelcome, "Kiss a sclate stane (slate) and that winna slaver you", "Kissin's cried doun since the shakkin o hands"; whether the young ladies adhere rigorously to this dictum is of course another matter; as another proverb puts it, "Dae as the lasses dae, say 'Na', and tak it". The unromantic husband says, "A kiss and a sup cauld water's a wersh disjune (insipid breakfast)". As almost everywhere as well as in Scotland, the processes of law are looked upon as an expensive snare to be most sedulously avoided: "Law is costly—tak a pint and gree"; laziness is hit off by the sarcasm, "Ye'll dae onything but work and rin eirands"; even in love moderation is to be aimed at: "Cauld cules the luve that kindles ower het", "Lue (love) me little and lue me lang".

For the canny man, patience and long-suffering is naturally a virtue, gone are the days of *Nemo me impune lacesset* and *praefervidum ingenium Scotorum;* one must endure to the

6

end: "Dree (endure) out the inch as ye hae dune the span"; and there are plenty of proverbs teaching him prudence both in action and speech, prudence being in this context basically self-interest, as in "Dinna meddle wi the deil and the laird's bairns", especially presumably if you are one of the baronial tenants; "Dinna scaud your mouth wi ither folk's kail (broth)", a more homely way of saying "Mind your own business"; "Dinna sell your hen in a rainy day", and one of the best known and a favourite of Sir Walter Scott, "Keep your ain fish-guts to your ain sca-maws", i.e. in English, "Charity begins at home".

As for discretion in speech, "Silence is golden" is one of the oldest and most wide-spread of proverbs. Scots ways of putting it are, "Aa that's said in the kitchen, sudna be tauld in the ha" and "He kens muckle that kens when to speak, but far mair that kens when to haud his tongue"; and yet it is not always so; "A man may haud his tongue in an ill time"; under sorrow, cynicism and self-interest again unite in "O aa sorrows a fu sorrow is the best", on which Kelly comments, "Spoken when friends die and leave good legacies".

"A wilful man will have his way" is a common saying on obstinacy, for which the Scots equivalent is probably even better known, "He that will to Cupar, maun to Cupar", which presumably originated in Fife; and on wisdom we are told that "A wife is wise eneuch that kens her guidman's breeks frae her ain kirtle." Says Kelly, "She is a good wife who knows the true measure of the husband's authority and her obedience". In these modern days comment would certainly be superfluous and injudicious. But wisdom is not always easily acquired, and a Scots proverb of the later 16th century tells against ourselves that "A Scotsman is aye wise ahint the hand (after the event)". Our political history in the past few years suggests that we have learned little since.

The other characteristic features of a proverb are manifested in their form. Because proverbs are chiefly handed down from one generation to another by word of mouth, from parents or perhaps more frequently grandparents to the children, they are more easily remembered if they are short: "The mair the merrier; dirt bodes (is a token of) luck; tak help at your elbows; a Hieland welcome; tyne (lose) hert, tyne aa;

7

your een's your merchant; hae (here), lad, and rin, lad; sune as syne (the sooner the better)".

Figures of speech and style help in the process, as through rhyme: "Bide weel, betide weel; monie haws, monie snaws; better rue sit than rue flit; learn ere (early), learn fair;" sometimes there is a whole verse, especially in geographical and weather proverbs, as the well-known "Carrick for a man, Kyle for a coo, Cunningham for corn and bere (barley), and Galloway for oo"; "East and Wast, the sign o a blast; North and South, the sign o a drouth", of the direction of the wind; or assonance: "Bode (aim for) a robe and wear it, bode a sark and bear it; do or die; giff-gaff (give and take) maks guid friends; tak tent (heed) o time ere time be tint"; or by one of the oldest devices of all, alliteration, as in the last two examples and in very many more: "Fuils are fond o flittin; jouk and let the jaw gae by; kame seindle, kame sair; tak the bit wi the buffet; better a wee bus (bush) than nae bield (shelter); cadgers are aye crackin o cruik saiddles; lat the saw (ointment) sink to the sair; ye shape shune by your ain shauchled (shambling) feet". All these are helps to the memory in retaining the encapsulated truth.

Balance and antithesis are others, whereby opposite notions are brought together to emphasise the contrast, like "Aft ettle (aim), whiles hit; lippen (trust) to me but luik to yoursel; a tume purse maks a blate (backward) merchant; better a tume house than an ill tenant; narrowly gaithert and widely spent; it's the belly that keeps the back up; guid gear gangs in sma bouk (bulk); ye breed o the leek, ye hae a white heid and a green tail", spoken, as Kelly puts it, to "old, graceless, profane persons" with a proclivity in one particular direction.

Punning is frequent, as in "Ye come o the house o Harletillim", i.e. you are a miserly gear-gatherer, harling (raking) in whatever is to be had; or "They aye gang frae Auchterless to Auchtermair", often used of ministers who were always on the lookout for a more profitable parish and a higher stipend. A similar jibe is contained in the saying, "Ye're like the minister o Bellie (in Moray), aye preachin for sellie (self)", or in general, "Ye come o the MacTaks and no the MacGies".

Nor is the note of sardonic irony absent from the proverb; "She's better than she's bonnie" is a very left-handed compliment to pay to a lady; "I hope ye're nane the waur o your early risin" is said to those who lie long abed, and in a like vein, "Ye're sair fashed haudin naething thegither"; "He's a guid man when there's nae better by", and "He's as welcome as water in a riven ship" are not exactly expressions of praise.

Because of their popular traditional nature proverbs tend to be formulaic, i.e. are couched in a set form with a phraseology or figure of speech or word order which is repeated from one proverb to another. The simile is of course common: "like water aff a deuk's back", "like a cried fair", "as plain as a pike-staff", "as fu as a puggie (monkey)", a gloss to the simile being often added, as in "like Royal Charlie, lang o comin", or "like the Hielandman's gun, that needed a new lock, a new stock and a new barrel"; the expression is often directly personalised, as "He's like a fish out of water", "Ye're like a hen on a het girdle", "Ye're like an ill shillin, ye'll come back again", a succinct popular version of Gresham's Law in economics.

An equivalent formula, common in proverbs from the 17th century or earlier, begins with the old verb 'breid', to resemble, take after; "Ye breid o Saughton swine, your neb's never out o an ill turn", "Ye breid o the guidman's mither, ye're aye in the wey". Another formula is expressed as a predication achieving extra emphasis by inverted word-order: "It's a ..., he's a ..., aa is no ... that ...", as "It's a guid tongue that says nae ill", "He's a wise bairn that kens his ain father", "Aa's no ill that's ill like". Comparisons or antitheses, as we have seen, are frequently in condensed form, especially in the type "Better gang farther than fare waur", "The nearer the kirk the farer frae grace".

Several proverbs link "fuils and bairns", as in "Fuils and bairns never ken when they are weel aff". A common formula is to express an impossibility or a paradox as an unfulfilled condition, "Gin aa stories be true, that ane's nae lie", "If the lift fa, the laverocks (larks) will be smuired (smothered)", and many begin with "It's ill" followed by a verbal noun, as "It's ill takin the breeks aff a Hielandman".

One special type of proverb consists in the quotation of a saying, followed by a designation of the person who said it and the occasion on which it was said, the usual formula being "As so-and-so said when ...", so that it is a mixture of quotation and anecdote, the anecdote thus being frequently etiological, as the learned put it, or giving an explanation of the origin of the proverb itself. It is now generally held that all proverbs, despite their common, indeed universal elements, began as independent creations, each one by some individual on some particular occasion, and whether the anecdote about its origin may be true or not, it is at least accepted as the way in which the proverb has come about. Dickens seized on this type of proverb in his picture of Sam Weller and his father in *Pickwick Papers*, and hence it has sometimes been called a Wellerism.

Here are some examples, and it will be noticed that not a few frame the saying in ludicrous setting, which some scholars see as a sign that the saying is much earlier than the accompanying anecdote, which may well have been added by some later humorist to dramatise the moral. " 'A clean thing's kindly (agreeable)', quo the wife when she turned her sark efter a month's wear"; the same wife no doubt as the one who said, " 'Lang straes are nae motes', when she hauled the cat out o the kirn (churn)", and presumably the wife of the man who said, " 'There's a mote in't', when he swallowed the dish-clout", and a near relative of the heroine of the other anecdote, "You're as braw as Bink's wife, when she beckit to the minister wi the dish-clout on her heid".

It was obviously a Scottish proverb-monger who had a dig at our legal system when he added to the common saying, "There's nae place like hame" ... "quo the deil when he fand himsel in the Court o Session". Even dogs may be quoted, like the one who said, " 'There's baith meat and music here', when he ate the piper's bag", and the kae (jackdaw) of Cambusnethan on the Clyde who said "Wae worth ill company", though Kelly tells us he learned it from a guest in the laird's house who was in the depths of a hangover. Kelly indeed has many quaint explanations for some of his proverbs, as " 'It's just as it fas', said the wooer to the maid", to which he adds, "That is, as my affairs and circumstances allow. It took its rise from a courtier who went to court a maid; she was dressing supper with a drop at her nose, and she asked him if he would stay all night; he answered, Just as it falls, meaning if the drop fell among the meat, he would go, if it fell by, he would stay". To which we may reply with another proverb, "Gin aa stories be true, that ane's nae lie".

Historical Proverbs

Some of these sayings are ascribed to specifically named persons: "God be wi the guid laird o Balmaghie, for he ne'er tuik mair frae a puir man than what he had", obviously a saying of radical tendencies, like " 'God keep ill gear out o my hands; for if my hands ance get it, my hert will ne'er pairt wi't', sae prayed the guid Earl of Eglinton", another of whose prayers was the cynically realist one, "God send us siller for they're little thocht o that want it". Kelly says this Earl was so mean that he sacked his chaplain and said family prayers himself. "Every man for himself" is a universal saying; the earliest Scots version, that of Fergusson of the late 16th century, adds "quo Saint Martin"; Kelly's Collection of 1721 puts it thus: "Every man for his ain hand, as John Jelly focht"; later still there is another version, "as Henry Wynd said", and a Gaelic version says, "Air a laimh fhein, mar a bha 'n ceard 's a'chaonnaig (For his own hand, as the smith was in the fight)". Scott, whose mind was stuffed full of Scots lore as few have been before or since, quotes the Henry Wynd version in *Rob Roy* and wrote a note to the effect that this Henry Wynd was a smith who, in the famous gladiatorial contest between the clans on the North Inch at Perth in 1392, volunteered to fight for Clan Chattan which was a man short in the thirty-a-side killing match. Eleven years later he worked the proverb up into the plot of *The Fair Maid of Perth*. Another more historical one is quoted by him in *The Fortunes of Nigel:* "He sits fu still that has a riven breek", which he ascribes, following Kelly, to the Earl of Douglas at the battle of Shrewsbury in 1403. The Earl, who was assisting in the rebellion of the Percies against Henry IV of England (see Shakespeare *Henry IV* Part i, Act 5), was wounded in his nether region, but gallantly sat still till his men's wounds were first attended to, and then announced his own by repeating the proverb.

11

Nearly two centuries later in 1583, on the earlier of the two rather mysterious occasions when the Ruthven family seized King James VI, then but 17 years old, and he burst into tears, the Master of Glamis repeated gruffly to him the old saying, "Better bairns greet nor beardit men". Then there is the proverbial reply of the border reiver John Armstrong, when pleading in vain for his life before King James V in 1529, "I hae askit grace at a graceless face", which is reported by several contemporary sources and is almost certainly the actual words uttered by him; and in similar circumstances, when the famous Jacobite Lord Lovat was waiting in the Tower of London for his execution, he heard that some scaffolding erected for spectators of the occasion had collapsed and killed several people, he repeated with that grim humour that marked his last hours the proverb "The mair mischief, the better sport".

The first principle of government is to establish what is now called law and order, or in mediaeval times more concretely and picturesquely, "to gar the key keep the castle and the rash bus keep the coo". It was apparently so enunciated first by King James I, but some later historians ascribe it to James II and others to James V, suggesting that it may have become a byword in the House of Stewart, handed on from father to son, though not always successfully achieved.

Folk-life in the Proverb

It is not only the dramatic episodes of Scottish history that are made memorable in our proverbs. Indeed the usual proverb mirrors far more the occupations and interests of the ordinary folk in their day-to-day life, especially, since most of our proverbs date from the early 19th century at the latest, the life of the village and the countryside and the basic activities of a rural community. Town life as such is seldom mentioned, and the metaphors and similes which so often mark the proverb are drawn from the rustic, homely, and familiar.

In the family itself the cycle of birth, marriage, and death is noted, for example, by "He's a fuil that mairries at Yuil, for when the bairn's to bear, the corn's to shear", which demonstrates the farmer's natural, unsentimental, and practical way of looking at things; like the other farmer whose greatest regret at his wife's death was that she had been inconsiderate enough to die in "the heid hurry o hairst".

The superstitions associated with birth are alluded to in "He was sweeled (swaddled) in his mither's sark-tail", said of a ladies' man, the procedure being to wrap a new-born male child in his mother's shift (or a daughter in her father's shirt), if he or she was to be successful with the other sex. If this proved not to be the case, then he must have been "keppit in a buird-claith (table-cloth)"; "He has some hap to his meat but nane to his wives", that is, he'll never be hungry but may never find a wife, or at least never a good one.

On the guileless indiscretions of children we have "Bairns and fuils speak at the cross what they hear at the fireside". A parent alert to this possibility might say to the company, "It's drappin suit (soot)", as a warning that the topic of conversation was taking a doubtful turn and should be dropped. On marriage, "It is better to mairry ower the midden than ower the muir", that is, among people you know than among strangers. As for the last of our mortal experiences, "Deith comes in and speirs nae questions", and so why worry? "There's remeid for aathing but stark deid", as Captain James Stewart is reputed to have said to the Earl of Morton, when laying the accusation of treason against him which led to his execution in 1581.

We are also reminded proverbially of the wife who with vain frugality "kept her supper for her breakfast and she was deid ere day"; and that leads us to the solemn reflection that "Our hindmaist gounie (last nightdress) has nae pouches", a truism already familiar to the mediaeval Italian, *"L'ultimo vestito ce lo fanno senza tasche"*. The homespun philosopher accepts it as the ultimate fact of life, and nothing more needs to be said. So he turns back to the business of living and gets on with the job nearest to hand for "Nae man has a tack (lease) o his life".

Food is the prerequisite of life, and without it we should not do very much; "A fu wame maks a straucht back", they say, or more commonly now, "It's the belly that keeps the back up", and the sign of physical well-being is to be "meatlike and

13

claithlike", well-fed and well-clad. Of one who is feckless and unlikely to make a go of it we still say, "He'll never mak saut til his kail (broth)". Kail incidentally is one of the staple diets in our proverbial menu, and an uneasy domestic situation lies behind the phrase "To get one's kail through the reek", i.e., to get a proper dressing-down, when the angry housewife serves up the food with a bitter-tasting garnish of vituperation. Reek, in this allusive sense, occurs in several proverbial sayings, as in "It's a sour reek where the guidwife dings (beats) the guidman", which Kelly in his inimitable way explains: "A man coming out of his house with tears on his cheeks was asked the occasion; he said there was a sour reek in the house; but upon further inquiry, it was found that his wife had beaten him". And today when some wag with the appropriate nods and winks says that his friend has "a reekin lum (chimney)", he is insinuating that he has a nagging wife. Another ironical remark in similar circumstances may be addressed to the hen-pecked husband driven out from his own fireside, "Ye're surely ower het at hame. "

In the matter of the specific articles of food, our ancestors' diet seems to have been plain enough. "Ae scone o a bakin is eneuch" is meant to inculcate contentment with small mercies; "The first fuff o the haggis is the bauldest" implies that novelty soon wears off; "Back to auld claes (clothes) and parritch" is back to simple living and the old humdrum after a spree; "Cauld kail het again", which has its origin in the classics, denotes insipid and wearisome repetition not only of food but of dull theological dogma or political clap-trap; but when you have got what you wanted and done quite well for yourself, then we say, "Your breid's baken", sometimes adding, "Ye may lay by the girdle" on which it was baked, no further effort being required.

The fire itself, with its old-fashioned swey and chain and pot-hook, has given us figurative expressions such as, "like the links o the cruik", of some very emaciated person; "to ding a hack (make a notch) in the cruik", to mark some special occasion or red-letter day; when the fire goes out, metaphorically as well as literally, we have "a cauld coal to blaw at", cold comford indeed; and there is one of those ludicrous "Wellerisms" in an 18th century proverb: " 'I never loved bout-gates (deviousness)', quo the guidwife when she harled (trailed) the guidman ower the fire".

One of the most domestic of proverbs is the common "like a hen on a het girdle", corresponding to the English "cat on hot bricks". The origin will be obvious to anyone who has seen a hot girdle put outside a farm kitchen door to cool and an inquisitive hen pecking the odd crumb off it while hopping from one foot to the other as each in turn gets uncomfortably hot.

The making of clothes was another of the goodwife's duties, and from that we get more sayings. "A knotless threid", which ran out of the needle-eye, was worse than useless, and a person who was equally feckless came to be so denominated. The lint or flax which made the linen cloth had to be dressed with a kind of steel-toothed comb called a "heckle", and "to be on hecklepins" is equivalent to the English "on tenterhooks" from the other trade of fulling. To wind the thread after it had been spun, bobbins were used, or pirns, as they are called in Scotland, and thence the proverbial metaphors about a "ravelled pirn, to wind a bonnie pirn, to redd a pirn", of difficulties one has deliberately or unwittingly created; and when one started at that point to anticipate the garment that was ultimately to be made, one might be "caukin (chalking) the claith ere the wab was in the lume", or in another rural metaphor, "counting one's chickens before they are hatched".

The other indispensable adjunct of the house besides the fire was the well as the source of water: "Ye never miss the water till the wall rins dry"; nor again, "Ye canna tak clean water out o a foul wall", that is to say, "You cannot gather figs of thistles" in Biblical phrase, or in the English proverb, "You cannot make a silk purse from a sow's ear". The tricky business of getting water out of a deep well with a pail is not always successful, and "lattin the tow gang wi the bucket" is another way of saying to write off one's losses, to take an irretrievable risk, to throw the whole business up, corresponding to the old English proverb, "To throw the helve after the hatchet".

We have met the midden already in phrases and sayings, but here are some more. Every farmer, even today in this chemical age, would agree that "The muck midden is the mither o the meal kist", if he still grows oats, which is doubtful; of a nosey interfering person it is said that "He's aye stickin his graip (fork) into somebody else's midden". Out in the fields the ploughman driving his team gives rise to the proverb, "Muckle whistlin but little redd (ploughed) land", or in English, "Much cry but little wool", a great song and dance about a small achievement; and from the commands to the animals to turn left or right comes the saying, "He'll neither hup nor wynd", of one who is obstinately perverse and intractable. Another metaphor from an unruly animal in the yoke is "To hae one's leg ower the harrows" or "To rin awa wi the harrows", applied to someone acting in an unrestrained manner in word or deed. "To owe someane a day in the hairst" is to be under an obligation to someone for previous help.

In the wider context of the parish or the estate, two of the chief institutions are the church and the mill, as the sources of spiritual and physical nourishment respectively, giving rise to the expression, "To mak a kirk and/or a mill o't", i.e. to make the best of a thing, to do what we can in the circumstances. There is a similar phrase in Swedish. The expression "kirk and market" covered all the public activities of the inhabitants (Burns in *The Twa Dogs* adds "mill or smiddie"); there was also the business of the travelling merchant or packman, recorded in the saying, "He has brocht his pack to the preens", i.e. has squandered his stock or his resources down to his last farthing. From the work of another traveller, the tinker, comes the expression, "He'll mak a spune or spill a horn", a non-committal observation on someone's abilities to make or mar. Unstinted praise is very seldom a feature of the proverb. The egg-merchant was another dubious figure: "He's no to creel eggs wi'' implies that you have got to watch him when he's buying and packing your eggs in his creel or basket. Other miscellaneous metaphors are "To set doun the barrow", to go bankrupt, fail in business, and "a bund seck and set by", applied to a betrothed person, bagged, tied up as it were, and set in store for the state of matrimony.

The animals about the house, the dog and especially the cat, figure in many proverbs. "To draw a strae afore the cat", to allure with false hopes, goes as far back as Henryson in the 15th century; "To learn the cat the road to the kirn", to teach bad habits which are only too easily learned, dates from the 18th; "A blate cat (lacking boldness) maks a proud mouse" from the 17th. Kelly's comment is, "When parents and masters are too mild and easy, it makes their children too saucy and impertinent"; obviously there was permissiveness in the air even then. The dog however is less amiable in "Bourdna (frolic not) wi Bawtie (a pet-name for a dog) or Bawtie will bite you", meaning there are some folk you mustn't take liberties with, a saying as old as *The Cherrie and the Slae*.

The farm animals are even more frequently the source of proverbs, like the cow in "Haud Taggie (a tag-tailed cow) by the tail", equivalent to the English "A bird in the hand is worth two in the bush" or in the Scots version, "worth twa fleein"; "There's aye some water whar the stirkie (steer) drouns"= "There's no smoke without fire"; "An ill-willie coo should hae short horns" is self-evident; "He ne'er tint a coo that grat (wept) for a groat" is applied to one who being careful in little will be even more careful in much; there is a rhyming aphorism about "The wifc's ac dochter and the man's ae coo, The tane is ne'er weel and the tither's ne'er fu", both being too much petted and fussed over; and then there is the noisy excitable person who is "like a coo in a fremd loanin (strange lane)", rather like, but not equivalent to, the English "like a bull in a china shop" or "a stranger in a strange land".

There's not so much attention paid to the horse, but he, or rather she, is given her say in " 'Sma sorrow at our pairtin', as the auld mear said to the broken cairt". Nor does the sheep play much part; "If ae sheep lowp ower the dyke, aa the lave (rest) will follow" has equivalents in English and other European languages, but it can be applied with peculiar appositeness to the Scots; "He thinks himsel nae sheepshank" is twice quoted by Burns, and corresponds to English "no small drink". It is however the pig that is the favourite butt of the proverb-maker, from the comical couplet, "The souter (cobbler) gae the soo a kiss, 'Humph', quo she, 'it's for my birse (bristles)' ", to the more sober-sided "As the soo fills, the draff sours", implying that abundance often leads to surfeit and hence to waste.

The ludicrous is again introduced in the simile "Like a soo playin on a trump (Jew's harp)", said of some very clumsy or ungainly action; or "It's ill makin a silk purse frae a soo's lug", to which Ramsay adds alliteratively, "or a toutin horn o a tod's (fox's) tail". And there is finally the now rather old-fashioned expression, "The swine's gane through it," meaning that the whole project (of any sort) has fallen through, originally of a marriage, from the old superstition that if a pig came between a lad and his lass, they would never be married.

Of wild creatures four are particularly noticed by our proverbial wiseacres, and in this area the proverb comes closest to the beast fable which has the same worldly wise ethos, and may possibly derive from it. One has only to recall the fables of Aesop from ancient Greece, but probably originating in the eastern Mediterranean, and the great mediaeval beast epic of Reynard, to realise that the fox is likely to be the "hero", if that is the right word, of many a proverb in all lands. Indeed to the fox are ascribed many of the qualities which are implicit in the proverb mentality—low cunning, realism, cynicism, resourcefulness, making the best of a bad job. Here are some Scottish examples, some also mediaeval: "The fox rins as lang as he has fit", which Henryson quotes in his *Fables;* "The tod's whalps are ill to tame" or, in an ironical version, "Tod's birds (cubs), ane guid, aa guid'', is a way of describing the effects of a bad breed and upbringing; ''The tod ne'er sped better than when he gaed his ain eirand'' is tantamount to saying if you want a job to be well done, do it yourself; self-interest is the greatest incentive.

The tod has been invariably given a bad character and the same is true of the corbie or raven, partly no doubt because the raven was sent out of the ark by Noah and did not return, giving rise to the expression "A corbie messenger" for one who fails to carry out his commissions. There is incidentally a weather saw differentiating the craw (rook) and the corbie: "The corbie says unto the craw, 'Johnnie, fling your plaid awa'; The craw says unto the corbie, 'Johnnie, fling your plaid about ye' ", that is, according to whether the raven or the rook is the first to call in the morning, it will be fine or bad weather. Another bird with a doubtful reputation was the gled or kite, which has now disappeared from Scotland. Its rapacity is characterised in the mediaeval phrase "greedy gled", and its habits are alluded to in similes like "Ye luik as if ye had faen frae the gleds", of one who looks ruffled, disordered, or shaken, as if he had just escaped from a bird of prey; and in the warning, "It's no for naething that the gled whistles", to be on one's guard as there is something afoot, "no smoke without fire" being more or less the English equivalent.

But it is probably the gowk (cuckoo) that has most caught the fancy of our proverbialists from the earliest times. "Efter this we will hear the gowk", from the 17th century, is as much as to say, "Well, what next?, nothing will surprise me now, wonders will never cease". A more modern version from the north-east uses another animal metaphor: "Ahint that, a cat in cuitikins (gaiters)". Another contemporary one is "Ye breid o the gowk, ye hae nae sang but ane." "To see the gowk in ane's sleep" contains a piece of old superstition that one's imagination ran riot after such a dream, and implies that a person has become extremely credulous or capricious. In Scotland the gowk is especially associated with April when it arrives; so "a gowk's eirand" is an April errand and "hunt-the-gowk" is April fool's day, in reference to the bird's elusiveness. "On the first day o Aprile, Hunt the gowk anither mile" is an old rhyme for the occasion.

The simple amusements of the country folk, their music and their dancing, are noticed in the jocular "Ye're as lang tunin your pipes as anither wad play a spring", of a dawdler; a person or thing indispensable to an undertaking is often described as "the stang o the trump", i.e., the tongue of the Jew's harp; *The Cherrie and the Slae* gives us the earliest example of "Tak a spring on your ain fiddle; ye'll dance til't afore ye're dune", a figure drawn from a rural ceilidh but used with minatory force as a proverb="take your own way, but you'll have to stand the consequences', a rather old-fashioned ethic nowadays. Another glimpse of the same is in the sarcasm to one who is a wet blanket or perverse or uncooperative, "Ye'll neither dance nor haud the candle" for others to see to dance. Golf has produced the expression "a teed ba" of a situation which is cut and dried and ready for one to exploit to the full, and for which another proverbial phrase is "to come to a peeled egg".

We might go on and on with examples of our Scottish proverbs all reflecting an old and nearly vanished society, a primarily agricultural community with a canny, down-to-earth and mildly cynical attitude to life and its problems and outward manifestations, and one might note in parenthesis the dearth of Scots proverbs from the sea and seafaring. No doubt because the proverb is an emanation of the people it is bound to mirror the social background which produced it, the same one that found its supreme poetic expression in Burns, and, as it happens, most of the proverbs still current go back to the 16th, 17th, 18th, and early 19th centuries before the industrial revolution had changed the face and later the ethos of Scotland. It is very doubtful whether the last hundred years have produced any new proverbs in Scotland, or indeed anywhere else in the industrialised west, though America is particularly fertile in new catch-words and clichés, gags and wisecracks, such as we might expect from a slick technocracy. But they are hardly proverbs in the sense in which we have been using the term.

Another reason for the decay of the Scots proverb lies in the decay of the Scots tongue, and its replacement by English among the very folk who once created them, but who have now lost the idiom which made them so pithy and racy. The old ones are less and less in currency, and even if they were, they would convey no meaning to the younger generation to whom they are addressed. And so an English one is used instead, if indeed a proverb is used at all. For proverbs themselves may be going out of fashion. They are in the main the vehicle of humdrum platitudes, prosaic philosophy, and unsensational common-sense, and their role grows smaller in our modern world of statistics and computerised knowledge and sophisticated theory, and the journalistic "expert", though the last at least still makes liberal use of the cliché when his "expertise" fails him!

Early Scots Proverbs

If we look back instead of forward, we can see that many of the earlier proverbs of the mediaeval period have a more aristocratic tone about them. The earthier, more plebeian proverb may to some extent stand in the same relation to the mediaeval sermon, homily, moral tale, allegory, fabliau and the rest, as according to one theory, that other genre of traditional folk-culture, the ballad, is likewise a popularised form of the mediaeval romance of the court minstrels and troubadours. As we have already seen, Henryson's poems are a prolific source of 15th-century proverbs.

Mediaeval proverbs tend to be more abstract and allegorical: "For it is said in proverb, 'But lawte (without loyalty) all uther vertewis ar nocht worth ane fle' ", echoing Barbour in *Brus*, "Leaute to luff (praise) is gretumly", and the more modern "The hert will never lie that's leal"; "An ill life, an ill end"; "Young bairns suld leir at auld men's schules"; "Be blyth in baill (trouble), for that is best remeid", says Henryson, for which the modern equivalent, as we have noted, is "Pit a stout hert to a stey brae"; "In your ain bow ye are owerschot" from *The Cherrie and the Slae* is like Shakespeare's "Hoist with your own petard". Again from the same source is "He that comes uncalled sits unserved"; "Faraway fouls hae fairest feathers" dates at least from the poet Dunbar; "A flier gets a follower" (from Henryson again) is explained by Kelly with some bluntness as "Girls run away to be pursued". "All hechtis (promises) suld be haldin (kept)", from 1450, is self-explanatory.

One of the earliest of our proverbs, dating from before the 15th century, is "Full hard is hungir in ane hale maw (healthy stomach)". Of misfortune Henryson says, "Off evill cummis war (worse), off war cummis werst of all", later reduced to "Ill comes on waur's back", or in English "It never rains but it pours". "That voyage never lucks (prospers) quhar ilkane hes ane vote" from *The Cherrie* has a surprisingly modern application. "A man's mind is a mirk mirror" is as early as Douglas's *Aeneis* of 1513. "No to lat the reek blaw on him", of an over-solicitous or pampering parent and his child, still in common use, goes back to the 15th century, "Shame is past the shed of your hair", in reference to "brass neck", to the mid 16th. "As sib as a sieve to a riddle" is found in Dunbar and his contemporaries, said of close friends who have everything in common. "A new tout on an auld horn", one of the best-known of Scottish sayings about an old story furbished up, "cauld kail het again" in other words, is met with in the 16th century. "To get baith the skaith and the scorn" is a common alliterative saying going back to *The Cherrie* and beyond, spoken, as Kelly vividly puts it, "when one gets a hurt and another laughs at it". "Falset (deceit) never made a fair hinderend" is adapted by Henryson but is never heard now, surprisingly enough, for it is as applicable today as ever it was. "It's nae time to lout (stoop) quhen the heid is aff" is an old metaphor from the days of the battle-axe and the two-handed sword; and another very old one comes from the harvest field, "Maistry (energy) maws the meadow doun", somewhat more forcible than English "Make hay while the sun shines", and interesting as being translated from a mediaeval French proverb. Scott quotes it again in *The Heart of Midlothian.*

Proverb Collections

Our Scottish proverbs therefore go back a long way, as far back indeed as our literature, to the 14th century. Henryson, as we have seen, makes liberal use of them in the 15th and Montgomerie in the 16th, and there is a short list of rhyming proverbs in the Bannatyne MS. of 1568. At the end of the century the minister of Dunfermline, David Fergusson, published the first printed collection of Scottish proverbs; the minister of North Berwick, James Carmichael, made another about 20 years later; Kelly made one of the best collections of about 3000 proverbs with useful notes and indexes published in London in 1721, but unfortunately, for the benefit of his English public, he drastically anglicised the text; in 1736 Allan Ramsay, the poet, issued his own collection, slightly smaller and leaning heavily on Kelly, but restoring his versions to their original Scots form.

A new and pretty comprehensive collection of more than 4000 proverbs, high and low, was made in 1832 by Andrew Henderson, a Glasgow painter, and in 1896 the largest of all, with about 5000 entries including rhymes, mottoes, slogans and local jingles, nicknames, historical sayings *et hoc genus omne,* was put together by Andrew Cheviot (Rev. J. H.

Watson) with an index and notes, useful and interesting as far
as they go, which is unfortunately not far enough. An up-to-
date and complete collection is a much-needed enterprise for
some professional paroemiologist (proverb editor for those who
restrict themselves to trisyllables or less).

Sir Walter Scott made prolific use of our familiar proverbs
and sayings and works them with great skill into the dialogue
of his novels, all to intensify the colouring of Scottish manners
which it was his chief purpose to depict. One thinks especially
of *Rob Roy, The Antiquary, Old Mortality,* and *The Heart of
Midlothian,* with *The Fortunes of Nigel* and *Redgauntlet* not
far behind. Shakespeare himself laces his plays with many a
proverb, not always recognised as such among the many
quotations of his own creation. And in much the same way
Burns and Scott have contributed not a few sayings which have
become such popular bywords among their fellow-countrymen
that they have graduated to the rank of proverb: "O wad some
po'er the giftie gie us, To see oursels as ithers see us", "Man's
inhumanity to man", "Foemen worthy of their steel", "It's no
fish ye're buyin, it's men's lives", "O what a tangled web we
weave when first we practise to deceive", are but a few examples. The rest will be found in their respective places below.

Local Sayings, etc.

We have already noted how many historical incidents and
speeches have found their way into our proverbs. Geography
makes its contribution too, and many places have some saying
attached to them. Aberdeen, as one might expect, has more
than its share of these, on whose truth or otherwise we are for-
tunately not called upon to commit ourselves; an old one hits at
their fickleness or unreliability, in "He's an Aberdeensman
that taks his word again (forswears himself)", or their complacency in "Tak awa Aberdeen and twal mile roun and far are
ye?", or their meanness in the riddle about the reason why
Aberdeen cats never drink cream, i.e. because they never get
the chance. The folk a few miles farther south are celebrated in
"I can dae what I dow (am able); the men o the Mearns can
dae nae mair", though why the Mearns should be so marked is

not clear; perhaps the alliteration with 'men' had as much to do with it as anything. Scott adopted the proverb in *The Black Dwarf*.

Falkland in Fife appears in two or three sayings, probably because it was the site of a royal palace and of the high jinks of courtiers: "Ye're queer folk no to be Falkland folk"; "Falkland bred" implies being courteous and well-mannered; and when people begin a work without proper tools or sufficient means they are to be deterred by reminding them that "It'll be lang or ye cut Falkland wuid wi a penknife". Another well-known saying, "It's a far cry to Lochawe" is a translation of the Gaelic "Is fad an éigh o Loch Odha", which is said to have originated in the battle of Glenlivet in 1594 when the Earl of Argyll, far from reinforcements from his own castle of Inveraray on Loch Awe, was severely defeated by the Gordons. So the moral is "Don't stick out your neck too far".

A year earlier another clan feud between the Johnstons and the Maxwells near Lockerbie in Dumfriesshire was such a savage affray that the Maxwells were finally driven off, with their faces hacked and slashed by the swords of their enemies; hence "a Lockerbie lick" for a severe face wound. The saying "Peebles for pleasure" is on the other hand quite modern, smelling somewhat of an advertising slogan by the tourist board, though it may well have been suggested by the mediaeval poem *Peblis to the Play*.

A common folk-tale motif of a drunk bewildered in a churchyard gives rise to the remark, "No to lippen to (not to be trusted), like the deid fowk o Earlston", when he noticed gaps between the tombstones and assumed that many of the occupants had risen and gone elsewhere. A more serious warning lies behind "Never misca a Gordon in the Raws o Strathbogie (Huntly, their home country)". Scores of places in fact have their local saying, and for a very comprehensive list the reader is referred to Cheviot's *Proverbs* and his index.

Localities lend themselves to epithets and nicknames, often bestowed by rival neighbours, and Scotland has plenty of these. But at this point we are beginning to stray beyond the bounds of the proverb proper. The best known is undoubtedly "Auld Reekie" for Edinburgh; "Seestu" used to be applied to Paisley from the notion that Paisley bodies, as they are still called, had a habit of ending their sentences with the word (=English 'seest thou', do you see?); "The Lang Toun" is Kirkcaldy, or, in Perthshire, Auchterarder; "The Muckle Toun" is Langholm, "The Bonnet Toun" Stewarton, "The Blue Toun" Peterhead, "St Johnstoun" Perth; natives of Selkirk are "Souters", shoemakers of the single-soled shoes for which the town was once noted; those of the rival town of Galashiels are "Sour Ploums", of Falkirk "Bairns", and of Forfar "Louns", of the men; Buchan men are "humlies", Angus men "doddies", both words originally describing hornless cattle, specifically the Aberdeen-Angus breed. "Gutterbluids" are natives of any particular place, now especially of Peebles.

"A Lammermuir lion" is the beast you would expect to find most frequently in the uplands of East Lothian and the Merse, a sheep no less; in England they are called sometimes Essex or Cotswold lions; "A Paisley screwdriver" is a Glasgow term for a hammer, implying that Paisley joiners have the unprofessional habit of bashing the screw like a nail rather than twisting it round and round in the slower and more laborious manner; in Paisley they return the compliment by calling a hammer "a Glesca screwdriver". And so the banter goes on in every corner of Scotland. About what is said or shouted to visiting teams at football matches perhaps the less said the better, even if it were printable.

The list of proverbs which follows is of course a mere selection of the better known ones, with some explanations added if they have not already been treated above. A list of greetings and common courtesies has also been appended, following Kelly who has a similar list for the 18th century. It should be noted furthermore that with a few exceptions the proverbs are those peculiar to or at least in commoner use in Scotland. Where a proverb or saying is current in Britain as a whole, as "To buy a pig in a poke" or "To keep a dog and bark oneself", "No fool like an old fool", "As poor as a church mouse", "Better half a loaf than no bread", "Faint heart ne'er won fair lady", or where the difference is merely in the use of a Scots word for its English equivalent, as in "The pruif o the puddin's the preein o't", "A flittin stane gaithers nae fog", "To creish one's luif", it has been omitted and readers may fail for that reason to find their favourites. There are however many expressions with the same meaning, where Scots differs from English in employing a different metaphor, of which one or two examples have been mentioned above, and a fuller list of these has been appended to the proverbs below.

Throughout this book incidentally some attempt has been made to render the text of the proverbs in a standard Scots form.

The arrangement follows the alphabetical order of the main word or phrase in the proverb.

A Selection of Proverbs

He's an Aberdeensman, takin his word again. *i.e. who retracts his promise.* (*a.* 1600)

For the same reason that the Aberdeen cats never drink cream. *i.e. because they never get the chance.* (Current)

Tak awa Aberdeen and twal mile round and far are ye? (Current)

What folk disna ken, disna anger them, *i.e. where ignorance is bliss.* (Current)

They aye gang frae Auchterless to Auchtermair. *i.e. are always on the make.* (Current)

The Auld Ane, the Auld Chiel, Auld Cluitie, the Auld Evermair, the Auld Guidman, Auld Hangie, Auld Hornie, Auld Nick, Auld Sandie, Auld Sautie, Auld Simmie, The Auld Smith, Auld *Suitie*, The Auld Thief, Auld Waghorn. All nicknames for the Devil.

Sooty

Back to auld claes and parritch. (Current)

The Auld Kirk. *The Church of Scotland; also jocularly for whisky.* (Current)

There is an end of an auld sang. (16th cent.) Memorable as having been quoted by the Earl of Seafield, the Scottish Chancellor, when signing the

Act of Union in the last Scottish Parliament in 1707.

Ance Provost aye my Lord. Scott *Redgauntlet* xx.

Barley   Ayrshire Proverb: Carrick for a man, Kyle for a coo, Cunningham for corn and *bere*, and Galloway for woo.

B

Aa's fair at the ba o Scone. *i.e. no holds barred.* Statistical Account of Scone in Perthshire (1798) XVIII 89: "In the course of the play (in the annual football match between the married men and the bachelors of the parish) one might always see some scene of violence between the parties".

The back o beyont. Quoted by Scott *Antiquary* ii. In Angus they sometimes add "far the gray mear foaled the fiddler".

Wi his back at the wa. *i.e. at bay.* (*a.* 1535). General Haig's famous despatch in April 1918 began, "With our backs at the wall and believing in the justice of our cause."

The back o my hand to you. *i.e. go to the devil!* (1768) Also in Irish.

He has aa his back teeth. *i.e. There are no flies on him.* (Current)

To bite the bairns. *i.e. to repay good with ill, behave ungraciously.* (1729)

easy to dress   The bairn is *eith to busk* that is unborn. Henryson *Swallow* 143. *i.e. Anticipation is often more pleasant than the actuality.*

Scots Saws

Young bairns sud learn at auld men's schuils. *King Hart* (1500)

Better bairns greit nor beardit men. (*a.* 1582)

Bairns and fuils speak at the cross what they hear at the ingleside. (1896) Kelly: The bairn speaks in the fields what he heard by the *flett*=Eng. (1640) The child says nothing but what it heard by the fire.

fireside

They were scant o bairns that brocht you up. (1832)

God is kind to fu folk and bairns. (1832) Similarly in English.

Your breid/bannock's baken. (Current) Kelly adds: You may lay by the girdle.

Brig o Balgownie, *wicht*'s your wa, wi a wife's ae son and a mear's ae foal, Doun ye sall fa. A prophecy on the old bridge of Don at Aberdeen, quoted by Byron, with black for wicht, in *Don Juan* X. xviii.

strong

They wad gar ye trow that ae thing's twa, and your lug half a bannock. (1818) Of confidence tricksters.

It's no *sonsie* to meet a bare fit in the mornin. (1721) An old superstition.

lucky

It's a bare muir that ye gang through and no get a heather *cow*. (*a.* 1600) *English: It's a long lane that has no turning.*

tuft

Put out your *barm* whaur ye tuik in your ale. *i.e. vent your spleen on the person who annoyed you.* (1825)

yeast

To tak the bree wi the barm. *i.e. to take the rough with the smooth.* (Current)

He's set doun the barra. *i.e. has become bankrupt.* (Current) *cattle tracks* Mak nae *bawks* o guid bere land. (*a.* 1600) Kelly: Spoken when it is proposed to marry the youngest daughter before the eldest.

To luik at baith sides o a bawbee. *i.e. before deciding to spend it.* Scott *Heart of Midlothian* xxxii. (Current)

To have a bee in one's bonnet. (Current) Cf. Douglas *Aeneis* Prologue viii: With heid full of beis. *i.e. whimsies.*

Ye're like the minister o Bellie, preachin for sellie. A Moray proverb from the early 19th century.

Better belly burst than guid meat spilt. (*a.* 1628 and still current)

It's the belly that keeps the back up. (Current) An earlier form is in Kelly: A fu wame maks a stiff back.

Ilka man wears his belt his ain gate. Kelly: an apology for a man's acting differently from others. Quoted by Burns in letter to G. Thomson, 1 Sept. 1793, and by Scott *Heart of Midlothian* xxxv.

offers Ye'll get waur *bodes or before* Beltane. (1721) *Don't refuse a reasonable offer.*

bush He's no the berry nor yet the *bus* it grew on. (Current) *English: He's not the clean potato.*

There's no muckle to rake efter the besom.

She's better than she's bonnie. (1721) Still used somewhat ironically.

Bide weel, betide weel. The earlier form (*a.* 1600) was: Weill bydes, weill betydes. *i.e. Everything comes to him who waits.*

shelter Better a wee bus than nae *bield*. (1721) Burns's took this for his motto. English: *Any port in a storm.*

Scots Saws

For *faut* o wise men fuils sit on *binks*. (*a*. 1600) Pro-   *want ... benches*
bably adapted from the refrain of Henryson's *The
Want of Wyse Men*, itself a rehandling of a common mediaeval theme which goes back to the Wisdom of Solomon and the book of *Ecclesiastes*.
Never truer than today.

Ye're as braw as Bink's wife when she beckit to the
minister wi the dish-clout on her heid. (1721)

As bare as the birk at Yule e'en. *i.e. in absolute
penury or indigence*. Alluded to by Montgomerie
Flyting (*a*. 1585) 436 and still current.

A laid abune a *birn*. *i.e. piling it on, the last straw*.   *burden*
(1706 and still current in North-east Scotland).

It's a hard warld that winna gie us a bit and a *brat*.   *rag of clothing*
(1721) Kelly: If a man be industrious and honest,
he can hardly miss food and raiment. Cf. Burns *To
Dr Blacklock:* They maun hae brose and brats o
duddies.

Tak the bit and the buffet. *i.e. the bad with the good*.
(1721) Scott also in *The Bride of Lammermoor* xxi.
Cf. Fergusson: I love not the bit and the buffet with
it.

Bitin and *scartin* is Scots folk's wooin. (*a*. 1600)   *scratching*
Squabbling being apparently a sign of affection
with us. Premarital psychology.

Ilka blade o girse keps its ain drap o dew. From the
refrain of James Ballantyne's song *Confide ye aye
in Providence c*. 1850, based on a remark made by a
poor woman.

A *blate* cat maks a proud mouse. (*a*. 1600)   *shy*

Shame fa the gear and the *blathrie* o't. (1721). Kelly: *trumpery*
The turn of an old Scottish song, spoken when a
handsome young girl marries an old man upon the
account of his wealth.

31

Ye're aye ready to blaw in his lug. *i.e. to flatter him.* (Current)

As happy as a bleck amang treacle. *Cf.* English: *as a sandman.* (Current)

Ye never ken whaur a blister may licht (when the sparks are fleein). (Current in North Scotland) Scott poeticised the idea in *The Lord of Isles* v. 18: O, many a shaft at random sent Finds mark the archer never meant.

sorrow Be blyth in *baill*, for that is best remeid. From Henryson *The Cock and the Fox* 125, the mediaeval equivalent of putting "a stout hert to a stey brae" (see below).

He daurna say 'Bo!' to your blanket. *i.e. Who is he to venture to reproach you?* (1721)

aim for *Bode* a robe and wear it; bode a sark and bear it. (1721). Now commonly in the form: Bode a silk goun and ye'll get a sleeve o't. *i.e. don't be too modest in your ambitions.*

farthing He wad rake hell for a *bodle.* (1832)

He will/winna rive his father's bonnet. (1825) English: *he will (not) fill his father's shoes.*

To let the bonnets/walkers gae by looking for the high hats/riders. (19th cent.) Of girls over ambitious in their matrimonial aspirations.

hooves "They're a bonnie pair," as the craw said o his legs/the deil said o his *cluits.* (1832) Also in Gaelic.

dressed A bonnie bride is sune *buskit* (and a short horse is sune wispit). (*a.* 1600)

trusts to lent (for unpaid service) fallow He that *lippens* to *bon* plows, his land will lie *ley.* (*a.* 1600) *Don't depend on promises of help.*

32

Scots Saws

Guid gear gangs in sma *bouk*. (19th cent.) *Much in little.*   *bulk*

It comes to the hand like the *boul* o a pint stoup. Especially to a practised drinker. Scott *Bride of Lammermoor* xi.   *handle*

Bourdna wi Bawtie (for fear that he bite you). (16th cent.) Cf. Montgomerie *Sonnets* lxii: Quhom Bawtie byts, he deir that bargan byis. On ill-timed banter cf. also: Bourd not with the gallows; Bourd rather with me nor my honour. (*a.* 1628)   *do not jest*

We'll ne'er bigg sandy *bourocks* thegither. (1736) *i.e. be friends.*   *sandcastles*

"I never loved *boutgates*", quo the guidwife when she haurled the guidman ower the fire. (1721) Kelly: The second part is added only to make it comical. No fun for the guidman though.   *roundabouts*

In your ain bow ye are owershot. Montgomerie *Cherrie and the Slae* 1101.

Set a stout hert to a *stey* brae. (1721) But alluded to by Montgomerie *Cherrie and The Slae* 484: Sic gettis ay as settis ay stout stomakis to the bray.   *steep*

His auld brass will buy a new pan. (1736) The young widow will soon get a new husband with her old one's money.

Hain at the *breird*. (19th cent.) *Be careful of the first profits.*   *use sparingly at the sprouting stage*

He left his siller in his ither breeks. (1832) *Of reluctant payers.*

It's ill takin the breeks aff a Hielandman. Scott *Rob Roy* xxvii. Rather less elegantly expressed in the 16th century without reference to Highlanders. (Current)

Man to man the warld o'er shall brithers be for aa that. Burns *A man's a man* v.

knocked about The best o him is *buffed*. (18th cent.) Scott *Pirate* xxxix. *i.e. he is past his best.*

A bund seck and set by. (1825) *Of a person engaged to be married.*

To make the rash bus keep the cow. Ascribed to the Stewart kings as the aim of their policy. See the introduction. Scott *Tales of a Grandfather* xxvii relates it of James V in his attempts to suppress border raids and thus allow cattle to be pastured unmolested and unguarded.

from one end of the house . . . in the other end It is ill to bring *but* that's no *thereben*. (*a.* 1560) One cannot produce what one has not or make bricks without straw.

gullet Like butter in the black dog's *hause*. (1721) i.e. past recovery, spilt milk. Scott *Antiquary* xxxviii, *Legend of Montrose* xv.

Ye're either aa dirt or aa butter. (1832) i.e. arouse extreme fondness or aversion.

C

Ca cannie. Current from the early 1800s. Galt uses it frequently. Also in expanded forms: and flee laich/ and ye'll brak nae graith.

pannier-saddles Cadgers are aye crackin o *cruik-saiddles*. (*a.* 1600) Always talking shop. Scott *Rob Roy* xxvi.

I will add a stone to your cairn. Pennant in his *Tour of Scotland in 1772* describes the practice in the Highlands of passers-by adding a stone to a memorial cairn erected for some deceased worthy as a mark of respect, and quotes the Gaelic equivalent, *Cuiridh mi clach air do charn.* But the origin probably lies in some primitive superstition about the need to confine the ghosts of the dead under a cairn of stones.

When the *cairrie* gaes wast, guid weather is past;   *cloud-motion*
When the cairrie gaes east, guid weather comes neist. An old weather saying from the east coast of Scotland.

It starts like a threid and ends up like a cairt-raip. (Current) Of gossip or rumour magnified in transmission.

Ye wad think ye had been brocht up in a cairt-shed. (Current) Of one who habitually leaves doors open.

There was never a cake but it had a *make.* (*a.* 1600) A   *companion,*
Berwickshire version puts it: Every bannock has its   *match*
maik but the bannock o Tollishill. Ascribed to the Earl of Lauderdale, who during his imprisonment in London under the Cromwell regime continued to receive his rent from his tenant at Tollishill in the Lammermuirs smuggled to him in a pease-bannock.

The land o cakes. (1669) A soubriquet for Scotland. Cf. Burns *On Grose's Peregrinations* i: Hear, Land o Cakes, and brither Scots.

As *caller* as a kail-blade. Scott *Antiquary* xxi.   *fresh*
English: *As fresh as a rose in June.*

Ye'll neither dance nor haud the candle. (1721) Of a recalcitrant person.

Pit canna in your pouch and try. (Current) Retort to one who says he cannot.

Ye hae a stalk o carl hemp in you. (1721) Of a dour stubborn person. Cf. Burns *To Dr Blacklock* viii. Thou stalk o carl-hemp in man (of firmness of purpose).

I'm ower auld a cat to draw a strae afore. (*a*. 1600 and current) Scott *Rob Roy* xxvi. Cf. Henryson *The Fox, Wolf and Cadger:* Thow wenis to draw the stra befoir the catt.

gaiters   Ahint that a cat in *cuitikins!* A North-east exclamation of surprise=Well, I never!

churn   To learn the cat the wey to the *kirn*. (1721) Kelly: an ill custom is soon learned. Scott *Monastery* xxxv.

coarse   As *course* as cat's dirt. (Current in the North-east) Very disagreeable.

A cauld coal to blaw at. (*a*. 1600) Offering little comfort or hope. Scott *Old Mortality* vii.

Cauld kail het again (is aye pat-tasted). (1629) The Greeks said: Twice cabbage is fatal.

bowl   My *caup*'s no aneath his ladle. (Current) *I'm not indebted to him or in his power.*

A causey saint and a house deil. (Current) English: *A saint abroad and a devil at home.*

chalking ...   Ye're *caukin* the claith ere the wab be in the *lume*.
loom   (1832) *Counting your chickens before they are hatched.*

trusts ... gap   He that *lippens* to chance lippens his back to a *slap*. (1832)

cudgels   Fuils sudna hae *chappin-sticks*. (*a*. 1600)

befal   He that cheats me aince, shame *fa* him; if he cheat me twice, shame fa me. (1736) *Once bitten, twice shy.*

dirtier   The *clartier* the cosier. Scott *Antiquary* xxvi, "their old sluttish proverb".

I'm no sae scant o clean pipes as to blaw wi a brunt
pipe stump   *cuttie*. (1721) Kelly: Spoken by a young girl, when they tell her of marrying a widower.

Scots Saws

'A clean thing's kindly' quo the wife, when she turned her sark efter a month's wear. (1832)

Ye canna tak clean water out o a foul wall. (Current)

A tongue that wad clip clouts. (Current) Of an interminable talker.

Gibbie's grace—deil claw the *clungest*. (1736) *An invitation to eat heartily.*   *hungriest*

On one's ain/anither's coat-tail. (1583) *At one's own or another's expense or effort.* Scott *Rob Roy* xix. (Current)

He aye keeps the *coble* heid doun the stream. *i.e. follows the tide.* Scott *Old Mortality* xlii.   *wherry*

To get one's meat in a riven *cog*. (1734) *i.e. to get a scolding, especially from one's wife.* Cf. *Kail* below.   *wooden dish*

Dae as the collier did when he met the deil, hae naething to say to him, if he has naething to say to you. (1896) Arising from a superstition that the devil waylays travellers and asks them questions which if they cannot answer will result in their being carried off. It is the theme of the ballad *The Fause Knicht upon the Road.*

'Come to the point', as the cat said when she let claut at the dog's nose.

Contentit wi little and cantie wi mair. Burns *Contented wi little* i.

An illwillie coo sud hae short horns. (*a.* 1600)

Like a coo in a *fremd/unco* loanin. (1721) Scott *Old Mortality* xiv. Of one utterly lost or bewildered.   *strange*

He ne'er tint a coo that *grat* for a groat. (1832) *By being careful in little things.*   *wept*

The wife's ae dochter and the man's ae coo. The tane is ne'er weel and the tither's ne'er fu. (1832) See Intro.

choke   To eat a coo and *worrie* on the tail. (1715) *To concede important things and object on trivialities.*

raven   Ye're a *corbie* messenger. (1450) Often quoted. See Intro.

The corbie says unto the craw, 'Johnnie, fling your plaid awa'; The craw says unto the corbie, 'Johnnie, fling your plaid about ye'. A 19th-century weather rhyme. See Intro.

Did ye hear the crack that that gae? (1832) *Said on hearing a great boast or manifest untruth.* (Current)

Ye hae a crap for aa corn (and a baggie for rye). (Current) English: *All is fish that comes to his net.*

That will never craw in your crap. (1) *You will never smell that;* (2) *That will never redound to your discredit.* (Current)

Sittin like a craw in a mist. *i.e. forlorn-looking.* (Current)

clear   To *redd* one's crap. (Current) *To unburden oneself of information, feelings; etc.*

To be in a creel. (Current) *i.e. in a state of great confusion or perplexity.* (*a.* 1600) Burns *To W. Simpson* iii, Scott *Old Mortality* vi.

He's no to creel eggs wi. (1825) *i.e. not to be trusted.* See Intro.

To keep the croun o the causey. *i.e. to be in good esteem and respect, to carry one's head high.* (1635) Rutherford *Letters* I. 149: Truth will yet keep the crown of the causey in Scotland. So there's still hope.

Scots Saws

Naething sae *crouse* as a new-born louse. (*a.* 1600)   *cocky*
  Kelly: Spoken of them who have been ragged and
  dirty and are proud. Rags to riches.

To pit a hack in the *cruik*. (19th cent.) See Hag.   *pot-hook*
  (Current)

Líke the links o the cruik. (Current in the North-east)
  i.e. emaciated.

The wife's aye welcome that comes wi a cruikit *oxter*.   *armpit*
  i.e. carrying a substantial dowry. (1832)

To haud the *cuddie* reekin. (Current) English: *To*   *horse, donkey*
  keep the pot boiling.

Lat him *cuil* and come til himsel (like McGibbon's   *cool*
  crowdie when he set it out at the window *bole*).   *hole, opening*
  (1721) Scott *Rob Roy* xxv. Now more commonly;
  Lat him cuil in the skin he het in.

Better out o the *cuits* than out o the fashion/out o   *ankles*
  kind. (Current) Earlier versions are: Better be deid
  (*a.* 1600)/out o the warld (1736)

I'll mak your lungs ring like a Culross girdle.
  (Current) Culross in Fife was noted for its
  manufacture of girdles in the 18th century.

Cummer gae ye before, cummer gae ye, If ye will not   *gossip, female*
  gae before, cummer lat me. (16th cent.) A formula   *chum*
  used by witches in the steps of their dance, given in
  evidence in the North Berwick witch trial of 1591
  and recorded in his collection of proverbs by Carmichael who was a commissioner in the investi-
  gation of the case.

He that will to Cupar maun to Cupar. An aphorism on
  obstinacy. (1721 and still current) Scott *Antiquary*
  xlii.

The curse of Scotland. A cant name for the nine of
  diamonds at cards. Recorded from 1710. No con-

vincing explanation of the term has been given, the most plausible being that the card most resembles the arms of the Earl of Stair (nine gold diamonds on a blue saltire), who was execrated for his involvement in the massacre of Glencoe and his support of the Union of 1707.

stumpy spoon   It is better to sup wi a *cuttie* than want a spune. (1721)

D

lumps   Raw *dauds* mak fat lads. (1832) *An encouragement to eat heartily.*

being skittish ... dotty   Daffin and want o wit maks auld wives *donnart*. (1736) *There's no fool like an old fool.* An earlier version: Daffin dow naething. (*a.* 1600)

Ye're as daft as ye are days auld. (1736) Much the same as the above.

gate   As daft as a *yett* on a windy day. (19th cent.) Of a scatter-brained person.

Dammin and lavin is sicker fishin. (*a.* 1600) Kelly: An advice to prefer a sure gain, though small, to the prospect of a greater with uncertainty. A metaphor from river-poaching.

copulated with   Thy dame was *swyvit* or thou was born. (1420) A calculated insult to provoke a fight. Ascribed by Wyntoun VIII. 2048 to Wallace taunting an Englishman.

harvest   To owe one a day in *hairst*. Scott *Rob Roy* xxiii, *Redgauntlet* xviii. To be obliged to someone.

No to see daylicht til. (Current) *To be blind to a person's faults.*

Scots Saws

Deal sma and serve aa. (*a.* 1600) An exhortation against lavishness.

Naething like stark deid. (1721) Said by Kelly to have been uttered by Captain James Stewart against the Regent Morton when he accused him of high treason, a charge which led to Morton's execution in 1581.

Ye're feart for the deith ye'll never die/for the day ye'll never see. (Current)

Ye're no fed on *deif nits.* (*a.* 1628) Jocularly of a well-fed person.   *nuts without a kernel*

It'll be lang or the deil die by the dykeside. (*a.* 1600) Scott *Old Mortality* xli. Kelly: Spoken when we are told that some wicked person is like to die. Henryson probably alludes to the proverb in his fable of *The Fox, the Wolf and the Cadger:* Heir lyis the devill deid in ane dyke.

Ne'er gang to the deil wi a dishclout on your heid. (1721) Kelly: If you will be a knave be not in a trifle but in something of value. i.e. as well be hanged for a sheep as a lamb. Scott *Fortunes of Nigel* xiv.

The deil bides his day. (1721) See Intro.

Some say the deil's deid and buriet in Kirkcaldy, Some say he's risen again and danced the Hieland Laddie. (18th cent.) Said to be an anti-Jacobite rhyme.

Afore the deil gaes blind, and he's no bleir-eed yet. (1832) A retort when one promises to do a thing "soon".

Raise nae mair deils than ye're able to lay. (1736) Originally from witchcraft.

Deil speed the liears. Repartee, altercation, mutual scolding. Scott *Redgauntlet* Let. xi. First recorded in reference to Prince Charlie and his companions in hiding after Culloden.

41

I dout the deil drappit him in the bygaun. (Current)

There's naething got by delay but dirt and lang nails. (1832)

wipe your beak   Ye may *dicht your neb* and flie up. (17th cent.) An expression of derision or defiance. *Go and chase yourself.* (Current)

Do or die. First recorded in *Wallace* IV 593. Also in Henryson and Burns *Scots wha hae.*

We maun aa die when our day comes. Scott *St Ronan's Well* vii.

fleeting moments   Stown *dints* are sweetest. (16th cent.) Cf. *Proverbs* ix. 17.

thump   Ne'er draw a dirk when a *dunt* will do. (1838)

Mony a time I've gotten a dicht wi a touel but never a dab wi a dish-clout afore. (1721) Kelly: Spoken by saucy girls when one jeers them with an unworthy sweetheart.

tasteless breakfast   A kiss and a drink o water's but a *wersh disjune.* (1721) Kelly: Said by a girl when asked for a kiss. Demonstrations of affection don't fill the belly.

shut   *Dit* your mouth wi your meat. (1832) *i.e. Shut up!*

The mither never had a sang but her dochter had a verse o't. (Current) *Like mother, like daughter.*

Twa dochters and a back-door are three stark thieves. (*a.* 1600) Kelly: Daughters are expensive and back-doors give servants opportunity to purloin their master's goods.

I'm no sae scant o claith as to sole my hose wi a docken. (*a.* 1528) Kelly: The return of a haughty maid to them that tell her of an unworthy suitor.

Scots Saws

There's a dog in the wall. (1721) *There is something amiss.* See Whaup.

To fell twa dogs wi ae bane/stane. (17th cent.) English: *To kill two birds with one stone.*

Ye're like the dogs o Dunragit, ye winna bark unless ye hae your hinder end at the wa. (1832) *Only show fight when in a strong position.*

Dinna tak the doo *or* ye hae the doocot. (Current)   *ere*
Don't get married until you have a house to go to.

We aa come to *ae* door at nicht. (Current) A truism on   *one*
mortality.

I can dae what I *dow;* the men o the Mearns can dae   *am able*
nae mair. Scott *Black Dwarf* vi. See Intro.

Ilka man has his ain draff *pock* (though some hing   *sack . . . lower*
sider than ithers). (*a.* 1600) *We all have our own
troubles and weaknesses to bear.*

The house draps *suit*/There's a drap in the house.   *soot*
(Current) *Be careful what you say; walls have ears.*
See Intro.

Naething to dae but draw your chair in and sit doun.
(1832) *Of one who finds a home all ready and
waiting for him.* (Current)

You will drink before me. (1721) Kelly: You have just
said what I was going to say, which is a token that
you'll get the first drink.

They speak o my drinkin that never consider my
drouth. (1721) Cf. Charles Murray *The Miller
explains.*

He has drouned the miller. Scott *Antiquary* xxi.
English: *To put the miller's eye out. i.e. to give one
excess of something, now especially of overdiluting
one's drink.*

The drucken man/wife aye gets the drucken penny/ groat. (1832) *i.e. can always find the money for drink.*

puddle There's a *dub* at ilka door (and at some doors twa). (1832) *There's a skeleton in every cupboard.*

To cairry saut to Dysart (and puddins to Tranent). (*a.* 1600) English: *To carry coals to Newcastle.*

E

'God send us siller, for they're little thocht o that want it', quoth the Earl of Eglinton at his prayers. (17th cent.) See Intro.

I hope ye're nane the waur o your early risin. (1832) Ironical to a lie-a-bed.

He has an ee in his neck. (1832) Of a prudent wary person. Common in Galt.

To pit out one's ee. (Current) English: *To put one's nose out of joint.*

bless God *sain* your ee, man. (1721) Kelly: Spoken when you commend a thing without blessing it, which my countrymen cannot endure, thinking that thereby you will give the blink of an evil eye. If the person commending be an unworthy or inferior fellow, they will say, 'Deil be in your een and a pickle salt together'.

don't match Your een's *no marrows*. (1721) *You are not seeing properly.* (Current)

empty eggshell Better half egg than *tume dowp*. (*a* 1600) English: *Better a half loaf than no bread.*

Tak help at your elbows. (Current) *i.e. exert yourself.*

44

To keep elders' hours. (Current) *To go to bed betimes.*
Dating from the 18th century or earlier when kirk
elders patrolled the streets at 10 o'clock to empty
the taverns and supervise behaviour.

Ell and tell is guid merchandise. (1721) *i.e. ready*   *pay down*
money is best.

Ye hae gotten til your English. Scott *Rob Roy* xxxv. A
sarcasm on affectation in speech. Now seldom
used, affectation being the fashion.

To hae gotten round the mou wi an English dishclout.
As above. Affectation in speech is described
variously as speakin Kelvinside (Glasgow), Morn-
ingside/Portobello English/Comely Bank (Edinburgh), Dichty Water (Dundee), Albyn Place
(Aberdeen), panloaf, pink, wi a *boul* in his mou.   *marble*

Aft *ettle* whiles hit. (1736) An exhortaion to per-   *aim*
severance.

F

Facts are chiels that winna *ding*. Burns's version in *A*   *be beaten down*
Dream iv, of an 18th-century English proverb:
Facts are stubborn things.

We maun bigg our dykes wi the *fail* we hae. (Current)   *turf*
i.e. *cut our coat according to our cloth.*

Fair *fashions* are still best. (19th cent.)   *manners*

Fair gae they, fair come they, and aye their heels
hindmaist. (1721) Kelly: Originally applied to the
fairies. Now applied to disreputable persons with
whom the speaker wishes to have no dealings, i.e.
the sooner one sees their heels the better.

Fair guid een and fair guidday. (1814) A greeting
implying formal civility but nothing warmer, cool-
ness in one's relationships.

To be taen to the fair. (Current) *To be disconcerted or abashed, to be deceived.* English: *To be taken for a ride, led up the garden path.*

Ye're queer folk no to be Falkland folk. (18th cent. or earlier) A Fife saying about people who are ostentatiously polite or elegant. See Intro.

Lang or ye cut Falkland wuid wi a penknife. (1736) Said when people begin a work without proper resources.

Aff/out o/in the fang. (Current) *(Not) in the mood or humour for.* A metaphor from the suction of a water pump.

They gae far about that dinna meet on a day. (19th cent.) *i.e. the world is a small place.*

It is a far cry to Loch Awe. Scott *Legend of Montrose* xii. See Intro.

Far fouls hae fairest feathers. (15th cent.) Dunbar *To the King* v, Burns *The Five Carlins* xvi.

To fash one's beard/thoum. (1725) *To bother one's head.* (Current with thoum in spite of modern tonsorial fashions).

tassel   Nocht worth a *fass*. (15th cent.) Henryson *Want of Wyse Men* 47, Douglas *Aeneis* II. 151.

The mirth and fun grew fast and furious. Burns *Tam o Shanter* 12.

builds
begs   The father buys, the son *biggs*, the grandchild sells and his son *thigs*. (1721) A truism on 17th-century social and economic history, "a proverb much used in Lothian" (Kelly).

It were nae faut. (18th cent.) Used ironically when one "assumes undue importance, or affects a niceness or delicacy which one is supposed to have no claim to"

Scots Saws

(Jamieson's *Scottish Dictionary*). 'It were na faut but dirt were dear', applied to people who give themselves airs.

To fecht wi the wind/wi one's ain taes. (19th cent.) English: *To fight with one's own shadow, i.e. to be very disputatious or quarrelsome.*

What reck the *feid* whaur the friendship *dow* nocht. (*a.* 1600) Kelly: signifying our contempt of mean persons whose hatred we defy, and whose friendship we despise.

what matter ... feud ... avail

The langer we live we see the mair *ferlies*. (*a.* 1600) (Current)

wonders

It's either a *tod* or a fern bus. (*a.* 1600) Also in contemporary English, when the speaker cannot be bothered to be more precise. From an animal fable about a blind goose which could not distinguish the two.

fox

Gin I live anither year, I'll ca this year *fernyear.* (1721) *i.e. I'll turn over a new leaf, be more careful next time.*

last year

There is *fey* bluid in your heid. (17th cent.) *You must be mad.*

doomed

Tak a spring on your ain fiddle: ye'll dance til't afore ye're dune. (16th cent.) Montgomerie *Cherrie and Slae* lxvi, Scott *Guy Mannering* xxxvi, *Rob Roy* xxix, *i.e. take your own way and be hanged to you!*

As if one had fund a fiddle. (Current) *In a state of great glee, having had a pleasant surprise.*

They were never fain that fidged nor fu that lickit dishes. (1721) Kelly: Spoken when people shrug their shoulders as if it was a sign that they were not content.

Fill and *fesh* ben/mair. Scott *Rob Roy* vi. Descriptive of extravagant living. (Current)

fetch

aching Better a finger aff than aye *warkin*/waggin. (*a.* 1628) (Current with waggin) Also in mediaeval English with ache. *The moral is: cut your losses.*

Keep your ain fish-guts to your ain sea-maws. (1721) Scott *Antiquary* xv. (Current)

To gie someone up his fit. (19th cent.) *To scold or rebuke.* (Current)

sleepless Fleas and girnin wives are *waukrife* bedfellows. (1736) No further explanation needed.

Flee laich and flee lang. (Current) *Keep your ambition within bounds.*

Lat that flee stick to the wa. *When the dirt's dry it will rub out.* (18th cent.) Smollet *Reprisal* II. ii; Scott *Rob Roy* xxiii. (Current)

humour ... brawl It's better to *fleech* fules than to *flyte* wi them. (1736)

flyer Ane *flear* gets ane follower commonly. Henryson *The Wolf and the Wether* 123.

scare Your face wad *fley* the French. (Probably dating from the French wars of the 18th cent.)

Better rue sit than rue flit. (*a.* 1600) Kelly: Spoken to them that long to change masters, servants, houses, farms and the like.

Ne'er tak a forehammer to break an egg when ye can do it wi a penknife. (1721) Cf. English: *To crack a nut with a sledge-hammer.*

straight-forward Forth the gate. (Current) Of honest straight-forward dealing and conduct. Cf. Kelly: Out the high gate is ay fair play.

Ye hae ower foul feet to come sae far ben. (*a.* 1600) *i.e. you are getting above your station.*

Scots Saws

Ay rins the fox as lang as he has fit. Henryson *Trial of the Fox* 32, Dunbar *Epitaph on Donald Odhar* 47, Knox *History of the Reformation* I. 114.

He that luiks to *freits*, freits will follow him. (1721) It is repeated in some versions of the 16th-century ballad *Edom o Gordon*   *omens*

Better a *fremit* friend that a friend fremit. (1832)   *strange, estranged*

Friday flit, short time sit. (1832). Friday being universally an unlucky day.

I may weill sie my friend neid, But I will not sie him bleid. Pitscottie *Chronicles* XXII. xxix: It is ane auld saying in Scotland, of an incident during the campaign of the Lords of the Congregation (1559).

The thing that's *fristit's* no forgien. (16th cent.) Scott *Redgauntlet* xii.   *respited*

To find the frost. (18th cent.) *To run into difficulties generally of one's own making.* (Current)

O aa sorrows a fu sorrow is the best. (1721) See Intro.

Nae that fou, But just a drappie in our ee. Burns *Willie brewed a Peck* ii.

It's ill speakin atween a fu man and a fastin. (Current) In Pitscottie *Chronicles* XVIII. xx, relates it of an incident in 1451 and Scott quotes it in Wandering Willie's Tale in *Redgauntlet*. A variant in Fergusson: Thair is nothing betwix a bursten body and a hungered.

A fu man's leavins. (*a.* 1838). *i.e. little or nothing.*

Fuils and bairns sudna see half-dune wark. (1721 and still current)

Fuils and bairns never ken when they're weel aff. (Current)

manure   The maister's fit is the best *fulyie*. (1832) By constant
               supervision of the work and the workers.

G

parsimoniously   *Gair*-gaithert siller will no haud thegither; the heir
               will be careless, his wife maybe waur; Their weans
mud   will be fearless and fa in the *glaur*. (19th cent.) A
               rhyming variant of 'The father buys' above.

               A gangin fit's aye gettin (though it be but a thorn/
               thrissel or a broken tae). (*a*. 1600) (Current usually
               in the simple form)

sauce   Thy guse is guid, thy *gansel* sour as gall. Henryson
               The Twa Myss 184. Probably from a fable.

till   Gape *while* ye get it. Henryson *Practice of Medicine* i.
               Kelly: Spoken to those who expect a thing without
               reason. They may gape long enough.

               Gar wuid is ill to grow (Chuckie stanes are ill to
               chow). (1721) *People resent being 'garred' or
               coerced.*

               Lat ne'er your gear owergang you. (1720) *Don't
               become a slave to your wealth.*

so-so . . . alas   'Geyly' is *sing walloway's*' brither. (1721) Kelly:
               Indifferent is next to bad.

give and take   *Giff-gaff maks guid friends. (a.* 1600) Scott *Heart of
               Midlothian* xvi, *Legend of Montrose* xiii, etc.
               (Current)

hoop   To ca one's *gird* (20th cent.) *To get on with the job, do
               one's thing.*

Scots Saws

Girn when ye bind and lauch when ye *lowse*. (1721)   *grit the teeth ...*
Kelly: Bind your sacks with care and cunning and   *unbind*
at the journey's end you will laugh to see them all
safe and sound.

He girns like a sheep's heid in a pair o tangs. Scott
Redgauntlet Let. xi. Of a horrible leer.

Or the girse grow, the auld horse'll be deid. (Current)
Of an elderly father and a young son, or of hope
deferred. Common in mediaeval English and cf.
Shakespeare *Hamlet* III. ii. 359.

To glack one's mittens. (1733) *To force one's thumb
and fingers apart, by putting a bribe into one's
hand, to oil one's palm.*

To *cast the glaiks* in someone's een. (18th cent.) *To*   *dazzle*
delude, bamboozle. Scott *Heart of Midlothian* xii,
Fortunes of Nigel iii.

As if ane had faen frae the *gleds*. (1837) See Intro.   *kites*

It's no for naething that the gled whistles. (1721)
Kelly: People who officiously offer their services
may be suspected to have some selfish end in it. An
earlier version of the 17th century: It was for
something the piet peipit. A reference to the fable of
the magpie

Gleg in the uptak. (Current) *Astute, quick on the ball.*

There's a time to *gley* and a time to luik *even.*   *look*
(*a.* 1600) *On turning a blind eye.*   *sideways ...*
    straight

The *gule*, the Gordon and the hoodie-craw, Are the   *corn marigold*
three warst things that Moray eer saw. A historical
proverb of at least the 17th century. The Gordons
came to Moray in the 14th.

Ne'er misca a Gordon in the raws o Strathbogie. (18th
cent.) *i.e. in their home town of Huntly.*

cuckoo

Efter this we will hear the *gowk*. (*a.* 1628) *i.e. nothing would surprise me after this, an expression of incredulity.*

On the first o Aprile, Hunt the gowk anither mile. (17th cent.) A rhyme for April Fool's Day. See Intro.

Ye breed o the gowk; ye hae nae sang but ane/never a rhyme but ane. (*a.* 1600) Alluded to by Lyndsay *Papyngo* (1530) 1102.

To see the gowk in one's sleep. (1825) *To have illusions; also to have second thoughts on sleeping over a problem.*

A gowk's nest. (18th cent.) *A piece of folly, absurdity a mare's nest.*

A gowk's errand. (Current) *An April fool's errand, chasing a hare.*

To seek grace at a graceless face. (1530) See Intro.

To keep the banes green. (*a.* 1513) *To preserve one's youth.* Scott *St Ronan's Well* x.

I'm no sae green as I'm cabbage-luikin. (Current)

He taks a guid grip o Scotland. (Current) *Of someone with big flat feet.*

I ken my groats amang ither folk's kail. (*a.* 1600) *When one hears one's own words or ideas relayed by others.*

gooseberry

To lowp at it like a cock at a *grosart*. (18th cent.) Scott *St Ronan's Well* ii, *Redgauntlet* Let. xiiii, *i.e. with great eagerness.*

There's first guid ale and syne guid ale, And second ale and some Hinkskink and ploughmen's drink And scour-the-gate and trim. (19th cent.) The names of the runs of liquor from the strongest to the weakest produced in brewing.

'Oniething *sets* a guid face', quo the monkey wi the
  mutch on. (1896)

goes with

Guid gear in sma bouk. (Current) Said of a small but
  honest or capable person; *much in little.*

Aa are guid lasses but whaur dae the ill wives come
  frae? (1721) Originally mediaeval. Cf. *Bannatyne
  MS*. IV. 34.

He's a guid man when there's nae better by. (20th
  cent.)

It's a guid warld—if it haud. (1721) Kelly: Spoken to
  them who take their ease and pleasure now without
  respect to their future condition. Also in Gaelic.

Stickin gangsna by strenth but by guidin o the *gullie.*
  (1721) *Skill is better than force.*

*stabbing . . .
knife*

The rank is but the guinea stamp, The man's the gowd
  for aa that. Burns *A Man's a Man* i.

Gunpouther is hasty *eldin.* (1838) *Don't go to
  extremes.*

firewood

Ha *binks* are *slidder.* Henryson *The Wolf and the
  Wedder* 155. See Intro.

*benches ...
slippery*

Hae, lad, and rin, lad. (1721) Kelly: Give ready money
  for your service, and you will be sure to be well
  served. Another version is: 'Hae' will a deif man
  hear.

He had *haen* that to dae. (1825 and still current) *He
  was fated to do that.*

had

To strik a *hag* in the post. (16th cent.) Lyndsay *Satyre*
  4435. See Cruik.

notch

The first fuff o the haggis is aye the bauldest. (1835) *On the attractiveness of novelty.*

slapped

Ane maun lue a haggis weel eneuch that wadna hae the bag *blauded* in his teeth. (1736) *Suggests the converse of the above.*

A hair in one's neck. (15th cent.) Scott *Rob Roy* xxiii. *A weak spot in one of which others may take advantage, Achilles's heel.*

A hair to mak a tether o. (18th cent.) *A slight pretext to make a great fuss.*

head

He sud hae a hale *pow* that cas his neibour nittie *now*. (*a.* 1600) *People who live in glass houses, etc., pot and kettle.*

Every man for his ain hand, as John Jelly focht. See Intro.

luckpenny

I aince gae a dog *handsel* and he was hanged ere night. (*a.* 1862) *An excuse for not giving a tip as apparently it did more harm than good.*

wealthy

A hairy man's a *geary* man, but a hairy wife's a witch. (1832) *According to folk-belief a hairy man will be wealthy.*

When hard comes to hard. (17th cent.) *If the worst comes to the worst, when the crunch comes.*

Ye come o the house o Harletillim. (*a.* 1600) i.e. avaricious. See Intro.

brains

There's mair in his heid than his *harns*. (Current) *i.e. he is tipsy.*

To hae one's leg ower the harrows/To rin awa wi the harrows. Scott *Old Mortality* viii. *To let oneself go without restraint.*

Scots Saws

To draw (at) the cat harrow. (16th cent.) Lyndsay *Complaynt* 308. *To thwart one another, to double-cross. Probably from a game so called.*

Naething suld be dune in haste but grippin o fleas. (*a.* 1600)

Hastie was hanged but Speed-o-fit wan awa. (1832) A story with a moral.

He has nae *haud* in his hand. Galt *Annals of the Parish* xlvi. Of spendthrifts. (Current) — *restraint*

Ye are sair *fashed* haudin naething thegither. (1721) *Who so busy as those who have least do to?* — *bothered*

Neither to haud nor bind. Scott *St Ronan's Well* xv. Berserk. (Current)

Haud your hands aff ither folk's bairns till ye get some o your ain. (19th cent.)

Haud your hand, your father slew a *whaup*. (1838) *A taunt to someone who utters empty threats.* — *curlew*

Gaither the haws afore the snaws. Galt *Entail* 1. Against dilatoriness.

To set the heather on fire. Scott *Rob Roy* xxxv. English says Thames and the names of other rivers are used abroad. Scott himself may be responsible for heather.

Juist the auld hech-how. (1778) *The old jog-trot.*

All *hechtis* suld be haldin. Henryson *The Fox, the Wolf and the Husbandman* 46. Quhar thou hechtis, se thou hald. (15th cent.) *Keep your promises.* — *promises*

To be on heckle-pins. (18th cent. and still current) *On tenterhooks.*

55

To hae the heft and the blade baith in one's hand. (1768) *To have the whip-hand.*

An ye heed aa ye hear ye may eat aa ye see. (Current) *Don't be too credulous.*

palm Ye'll get your lug in your *luif*. (18th cent. Used by Adam Smith) Now more commonly: Ye'll get your heid in your hands and your lugs to play wi'. *Of a severe reprimand.*

Their heid's no sair that did that. (Current) *They are no more.*

young pig To lay the heid o the soo to the tail o the *grice*. (1721) Kelly: Balance your loss with your gain. Scott *Rob Roy*, xxiv.

chimney What's held in at the door gangs out at the *lum/* window. (*a.* 1628) *On misdirected economy.* (Current)

Thou hell o aa diseases. Burns *Address to the Toothache* i.

Like a hen on a het girdle. (Current) Burns *Letter* (1787), Scott *Waverley* lxxi.) *Like a cat on hot bricks.*

He will not sell his hen on a rainy day. (*a.* 1687) *He gets the best of a bargain.*

It's a sairie/puir hen that canna scart for ae burd/ chicken. (1721). Kelly: Spoken of them that have but one child to provide for. (Current)

The hert aye's the pairt aye, That maks us richt or wrang. Burns *Epistle to Davie* v.

Better that ae hert brak than aa the warld winders. (Current) A Shetland proverb, *to keep one's sorrows to oneself.*

Ye're surely ower het at hame. (Current) See Intro.

Scots Saws

The hicht o nonsense is suppin sour milk wi an *elsin*.   *awl*
  (1832)

Ye fand it whaur the Hielandman fand the tangs.
  (*a.* 1600) *i.e. at the fireside, a euphemism for
  stealing.*

Your hindmaist *gounie* has nae pouches. (Current) A   *nightie*
  common proverb in most countries.

I have brocht you to the ring; *hop* gif ye can. Ascribed   *dance*
  to Wallace in addressing his troops before the
  battle of Falkirk, 1298.

Gae hop and hang yoursel and then ye'll die dancin.
  (1721) Kelly: An impertinent ill-mannered byword.
  Cf. Tak a spring on your ain fiddle.

He'll either mak a spune or spoil a horn. Scott *Rob
  Roy* xxii. *He will cut a figure in the world, hit or
  miss.* (Current)

Horse and *hattock*. (1662) Originally a rallying call   *little hat*
  by witches to mount their magic steeds for their
  sabbaths. 'Came to be familiarly applied on any
  occasion of mounting', Scott *Fair Maid of Perth* vii.

Huilie and fairlie (gangs far in a day). (*a.* 1600) Cf.   *gently*
  the mediaeval English 'Faire and softe me ferre
  gose.' The policy of Ca cannie.

Hunger is hard in a hail maw. (*a.* 1400) *Legend of
  Saints* I. 653, Wyntoun *Chronicles* II. 200. Cf. A fu
  man and a fastin above.

He'll neither *hup nor wynd*. (18th cent.) Scott *Old*   *turn right nor left*
  Mortality xxiii. See Intro.

J

Ill comes upon *waur's* back. (1721) Cf. Henryson   *worse*
  Trial of the Fox 10: Off evill cummis war, off war
  cummis werst of all. *It never rains but it pours.* Also
  Waur on waur's back. (Current)

'Wae worth ill companie', quo the kae o Camnethan. (1721) See Intro.

stamp She has an ill *paut* wi her hind fit. (1721) Kelly: Signifying that such and such a woman is stubborn.

He has an ill-scrapit tongue. (18th cent.) Scott *Rob Roy* xvii. Of a foul-mouthed malicious person. (Current)

reaper An ill *shearer* ne'er got a guid huik. (1721) *A bad workman always blames his tools.*

endure *Dree out* the inch as ye hae dune the span. (16th cent.) Montgomerie *A Counsel against Despair in Love*. Also in Fergusson, Carmichael, Henderson.

Man's inhumanity to man. Burns *Man was made to mourn* vii.

He suld weir iron schone, suld byd a man's deid. (*a.* 1568) *Waiting for dead men's shoes.*

J

There's as monie Johnstons as Jardines. (1832) A Dumfriesshire proverb, where these names are common. *Six of one and half a dozen of the other.*

Jedburgh *Jeddart* justice. *Punishment before conviction.* Ascribed to various instances of arbitrary justice done in the Border troubles in the late 16th century. England has similar expressions, e.g. Lydford law (1399).

He is but Jock the laird's brither. (17th cent.) See Intro.

To play Jock Needle Jock Preen. (*a.* 1628 and still current) *To play fast and loose.*

We're aa Jock Tamson's bairns. (Current) *Of common humanity.* The original Jock Tamson has not yet been traced. See the *Scottish National Dictionary* s.v. Jock, 4 (34).

The deil's gane ower Jock Wabster. (1725) *Hell has broken loose.* The original Jock Wabster also eludes us. Scott *Rob Roy* xiv.

Jouk and lat the jaw gae by. (1660) Kelly: Prudently yield to a present torrent. Scott *Rob Roy* xxv. (Current)

It's past joukin when the heid's aff. (*a.* 1600) Cf. Henryson *Preiching of the Swallow* 145: The nek to stoup quhen it the straik sall get, is sone eneuch. *Be ready to cope with trouble. It's too late to lock the stable door when the steed's stolen.*

He has a guid judgment that disna lippen til his ain. (Current) *Take advice.*

If a man's gaun doun the brae, ilka ane gies him a jundie. (1832) *On hitting a man when he is down.*   jostle

He eats his kail in a riven dish. (1721) Kelly: Spoken of them who are lightly regarded.

To gie ane his kail throu the reek. (1705) *To give one a severe rebuke.* See Intro. Scott *Old Mortality* xiv.

Ye're no worth cain out o a kailyard. (1832)

A pretty kettle of fish. From the Border practice of cooking salmon alive in boiling water, mentioned in the early 16th century.

lot, chance To count one's *kinch*. (*a.* 1585) Montgomerie *Cherrie and the Slae* 1100. *To form a just estimate of one's condition.*

bought Kindness comes o will; it canna be *coft*. (*a.* 1600)

way The king's eirand may come in the cadger's *gate*. (1721) Kelly: A great man may want a mean man's service. Scott *Fortunes of Nigel* xxvii.

A man may luve the kirk and yet no ride on the riggin o't. (1721) Scott *Redgauntlet* xiii. *No need for excessive demonstrations of zeal.*

To mak a kirk and/or a mill o't. (1721) *To do what one will or can with anything.* Galt *Entail* xviii. (Current)

Ye're no aye gaun to the kirk when ye gang doun the kirkgate. (Current)

thatch ... choir He rives the kirk to *theik* the *queir*. (*a.* 1600) *i.e. robs Peter to pay Paul.*

I'll kiss you when ye're sleepin. (1721 and current) A jocular promise of a reward for a favour.

As easy as kiss my luif. *A easy as winking.* Kiss-my-luiff also as an expression of disdain: I dinna gie a kiss-my-luif. (18th cent.)

Aa that's said in the kitchen sudna be tauld in the ha. (1737) Enjoining prudence in conversation.

ticklish ... shoe *Kittle* to *shae* ahint. (16th cent.) *Temperamental, difficult to manage.* Scott *Heart of Midlothian* xxxviii: Kings are kittle cattle to shoe behind. See next.

Women are kittle cattle; the mair ye rin efter them the mair they flee awa. (19th cent.) Kittle cattle is still in common use.

To be at the *knag* and the *widdie*. (19th cent.) *To be pulling in different directions, at loggerheads.* *peg … rope*

Like a knotless threid. (18th cent.) *Aimlessly, futilely, without purpose.*

Kythe in your ain colours (that folk may ken you). (*a.* 1600) *Come clean* *show yourself*

The kirk is muckle but ye may say mass in ae end o't. (*a.* 1628) Kelly: Spoken when people say something is too much, intimating that they need take no more than they have use for. Cf. Scott *Redgauntlet* Let. xiii.

L

Dinna meddle wi the deil and the laird's bairns. (1736) See Intro.

Ye luik like a Lammermuir lion. (1721) *i.e. a sheep.* English: an Essex lion, a Cotswold lion.

The land o the *leal* (18th cent.) Heaven. Best known from Lady Nairne's song, written about 1800. *faithful*

Ye've been lang on little *yird*. (1721) *You have little to show for your work*, a metaphor from ploughing. *earth*

Atween you and the lang day be it. (1721) Kelly: an appeal to the Day of Judgment. Scott *Redgauntlet* Let. xi.

Lang mint, little *dint*. (1721) Kelly: Spoken when men threaten much and dare not execute. *thump*

'Lang straes are nae motes' (quo the wife when she hauled the cat out o the kirn). (*a.* 1600) *Of something which is beyond a joke.*

Scots Saws

halter   Ye hae aye a fit out o the *langel*. (1721) *Of a fractious perverse person.*

Out o sicht out o languor. (*a.* 1628) English: *Out of sight out of mind.* (Current)

Dae as the lasses dae, say 'Na' and tak it. (1736) *Female logic.* (Current)

without   *But* lautie all uther virtues are nocht worth ane flie. Quoted in Henryson *The Fox, the Wolf and the Husbandman* 55. Loyalty is much praised in mediaeval Scottish poetry. Cf. Barbour *Brus* I. 16:
praise greatly   Leaute to *luff* is *gretumly.*

lark   It is better to hear the *laverock* sing than the mouse cheep. A motto for guerillas to keep as much as possible in the open, ascribed by Scott to the Douglases in the War of Independence, *Tales of a Grandfather* ix, *Fair Maid of Perth* xxx.

There's nae reek in the laverock's house. A Perthshire saying about a wild and windy night, adapted in a well-known lyric by Hugh MacDiarmid.

To be at the lug o the law. (1721) *At the centre of things, in close touch with authority.* (Current)

Show me the man and I'll show you the law. (*a.* 1600) In reference to bias in legal decisions. Scott *Bride of Lammermoor* ii.

Law's costly—tak a pint and gree. (1736) *i.e. settle out of court.*

tavern bill   Fair fa the wife and weel may she spin, That counts aye the *lawin* wi a pint to come in. (1736) *i.e. gives the last pint as discount.*

Leal hert lied never. (1768) Another aphorism on loyalty.

Ane leill man is nocht tane at half a taill. Henryson *The Fox, the Wolf and the Husbandman* 58. *Truth is not found by hearing only one side of a story.*

Scots Saws

Learn early, learn fair. (*a*. 1600) (Current)

Gin a lie could hae *worried* you, ye wad hae been deid lang syne. (1721) *choked*

Ye can tell that lie by the lenth o't. (20th cent.) *Truth is simpler than deceit.*

Ye breid o the leek, ye hae a white heid and a green tail. (1721) Of an old roué.

Left to anesel. (18th cent.) *Misguided, led astray in one's judgment.* (Current)

Let-a-be for let-a-be. *i.e. mutual tolerance.* Scott *Pirate* xxxvii. Michael Scott *Cruise of the Midge* ii. calls it Cathkin's covenant, from a laird of Cathkin who was accosted one night in his cups by a ghost but stood his ground, whereupon the ghost and he came to these terms.

Ye lick your lips or the pock be opened. (Current)

No to lippen to, like the deid folk o Earlston. See Intro.

Ye luik like a Lochaber aix. (*a*. 1600) *Of a startled look, with sharpened features.*

A Lockerbie lick. See Intro. (Current till the 19th cent.)

To lowp a gutter/stank dykes. (18th cent.) *To circumvent or surmount a difficulty.*

That voyage never luckis quhar ilke ane hes a vote. Montgomerie *Cherrie and Slae* li.

Your *luckie's mutch* (and *lingels* at it)! (19th cent.) *grannie's cap ... strings*
An expression of impatient contempt or incredulity, fiddlesticks! Also: Kiss your luckie, "when one thinks it is not worth while to give a direct answer" (Ramsay). Grannie is similarly used currently.

63

To lay one's lugs into. (Current) *To eat greedily, to wire into.* (1718)

Lue your friend but luik to yoursel. (1721) Now commonly: lippen to me but ... *Don't trust anyone too much.*

chimney   Glowerin in the *lum* never filled the pot. A Shetland saying.

It's easier to bigg lums than to keep them reekin. (1838) With similar application to the above.

Cauld cules the luve that kindles ower het. (1567)

Lue me little and lue me lang. (1838) A more modern version of the above. *Moderation in all things, even in love.*

M

Ye'll worry in the band, like MacEwan's calf. (1721) *i.e. you'll be hanged.*

MacFarlane's bouat/lantern. Scott *Waverley* xxxviii, and note: The clan of the MacFarlanes were great depredators on the Low Country and as their excursions were made usually by night, the moon was proverbially called their lantern.

Ye come o the MacTaks, no o the MacGies. (1832) See Intro.

I'll dae as MacKissock's coo. I'll think mair than I'll say. (1721) i.e. I'll watch my opportunity for retaliation. How the cow proceeded in the matter or who MacKissock was is not recorded.

wood   Ye'll no mak made *wuid*. (Current) Said of someone who is too old to be reformed.

Scots Saws

Aa arena maidens that wear bare hair. (*a.* 1600) From
the practice of unmarried girls wearing a *snuid* only   *hair-band*
without a hat or cap.

Mealy-moued maidens stand lang at the mill. (1736)
Don't be too coy.

Maidens' bairns (and bachelors' wives) are aye weel
bred. (1736) *Theory as opposed to practice.*
(Current)

Maidens' *tochers* and ministers' stipends are aye less   *dowries*
than they're caed. (1736)

Nineteen naesays o a maiden are half a grant.
(*a.* 1600) See under Lasses.

Maidens should be *mim* till they're married, and then   *prim*
they may burn kirks. (1721) Kelly: When we say
that such a one is a good-humoured girl, observe
how she'll prove when she is married.

He that invented the maiden first *handselled* it. (17th   *was the first to*
cent.) It is said that the Regent Morton introduced   *try*
a kind of guillotine into Scotland and himself died
by it in 1581, though not the first.

The mair they talk I'm kent the better. Burns *Address
to an Illegitimate Child* iii.

Marriage is a creel where ye maun catch an adder or
an eel. Galt *Entail* (1823) xxv.

Better woo/mairry ower the midden than ower the
muir. (*a.* 1600) *Better marry among those you
know than among strangers.* (Current)

Maisterfu folk maunna be *mensefu.* (1832)   *polite*

He will be a man afore his mither. (1721) Kelly:
Spoken to ill-grown children. (Current)

To blaw and haud meal in one's mouth. (1782) *To
uphold two irreconcilable policies.*

If you wantit me and your meat, ye wad want ae guid friend. (*a.* 1600) The second rather than the first.

good manners   I hae my meat and my *mense* baith. (*a.* 1628) Said by one whose offer of hospitality has been refused.

'There's baith meat and music here', quo the dog when he ate the piper's bag. (1832)

To be meat-like and claith-like. (1762 and current) *Well-fed and dressed.*

Fare ye weel, Meg Dorts, and e'en's ye like. Ramsay *Gentle Shepherd* I. i, who probably invented Meg Dorts. A riposte to one who goes off in the sulks. To *sulks*   tak the *dorts* (1637)

mallet   To keep the *mell* in the shaft. (18th cent.) Carlyle *Letters* (1831). *To keep one's affairs in good order and prosperity.*

There's no ane o them to mend anither. (Current) *One is as bad as the other.*

may   Men suld mak mirrie quhill they *moucht. Buke of Alexander* II. 224 (*c.* 1400)

'There's nae sin in a merry mind', as the auld wife said when she gaed whistlin ben the kirk on Sunday. (19th cent.) A more modern version of the above.

Your mind's aye chasin mice. (1736) *Your wits are wool-gathering.*

The best-laid schemes o mice and men gang aft agley. Burns *To a Mouse* vii.

'Mickle about ane,' quoth the deil to the collier. (1736) *Much of a muchness, both black and grimy.*

large size   *Mickledom* is nae virtue. (1721) *Small is beautiful.*

Had you no been in the midden you wadna hae seen that. (1721) Cf. Oven below.

Scots Saws

To glower at the mune and licht in the midden. (1721)
From having one's head in the clouds. (Current)

The muck midden is the mither o the meal kist. (1832)
Rural economy.

Ye wad mairry a midden for the muck. (1832) *Of
sordid greed.*

Aye stickin his *graip* in his neibour's midden.   *fork*
(Current) *Of a meddlesom tittle-tattling person.*

There's nae *breird* like midden breird. (1721) Kelly: *sprouting*
Spoken when we see people of mean birth rise
suddenly to wealth and honour. (Current)

There's aye a mids in the sea. (1721) *Moderation in
all things.* (Current)

He tells lies like a mill *shillin*. (19th cent.)   *separating husks*

As mim as a Mey puddock. (Current) Galt *Entail* III.
viii. From the superstition that frogs' mouths were
sealed in the month of May.

A man's mind is a mirk mirror. (1513) Douglas *Aeneis*
VIII. Prol.

The mair mischief, the better sport. (1721) Repeated
by Lord Lovat at his execution. See Intro.

Misery and mair makin ready. (Current) *Of a chapter
of accidents, one damned thing after another.*

The deil's greedy but ye're misleared. (19th cent. and
current)

A close mou maks a wise heid. (Current)

Moyen does mickle but money does mair. (1736) *Cf.*   *wire-pulling*
English: *Money is better than my Lord's letter.*

To tak a munelicht flittin. (1721) *To decamp without
paying one's debts.*

Aff at the nail. (1721 and current) Off one's head. Kelly: Taken from scissors when the two sides go asunder.

Narrowly gaithered and widely spent. (1721) Cf. 'The father buys' above. (Current)

My foot is on my native heath and my name is MacGregor. Scott *Rob Roy* xxxiv.

serves   If honest nature made you fools, What *sairs* your grammars? Burns *Epistle to J. Lapraik* xi.

clenched fist   He has as muckle sense as a hen could haud in her steekit *neive*. (*a.* 1835)

There's ower monie nicks in his horn for that. (1862) English: *He's too long in the tooth for that.* (Current)

cattle   Better sell *nowt* than sell nations. (1708) See Intro.

all one wool   To be *aa ae oo*. (18th cent.) English: To be birds of a feather. From the story of an imaginary conversation about wool in Scots conducted without any consonants, first noted by Ramsay in the glossary to his poems in 1721.

churn   If the auld wife hadna been in the oven hersel, she ne'er wad hae thocht o luikin for her dochter there. In 16th-century English. Scottified as: They socht me never in the *kirn* bot they that hes bene therein. (*a.* 1628)

Scots Saws

Aa *owers* are ill, but ower the water and ower the hill. (17th cent.) Cf. Montgomerie *Cherrie and Slae* 435: All ouirs are repuit to be vyce.
excesses

Wi one's heid under one's *oxter* (Current) *Downcast, crestfallen.*
armpit

P

Ye hae brocht the pack to the preens/pins. (16th cent. and current) Montgomerie *Cherrie and Slae* xciii. *You have squandered your resources.*

The pain owergangs the profit. (1736) *Of something not worth while.*

There wad be little parritch in your caup if he had the pourin o't. (Current)

The true pathos and sublime of human life. Burns *To Dr Blacklock* ix.

Hair like a pease-wisp. (19th cent. and current) *Tousled, shaggy, unkempt.*

Ye hae come to a peeled egg. (1721) Kelly: Spoken to those who have got an estate, place or preferment ready prepared for their hand, or as the English say, Cut and dry.

Nae friend like the penny. (1832) Cf. Moyen, Siller.

When petticoats woo, breeks may come speed. (1721) Kelly: Spoken when maids court young men.

Monie a *pickle* maks a mickle. (Current) A familiar proverb in all languages, but invariably misquoted in Scotland as "Monie a mickle maks a muckle".
grain

The *pig* gangs to the wall til ae day. (Current) *Everything perishes some day.*
pitcher

69

To gang to pigs and whistles. (17th cent.) *To go to pot.* (Current) Pigs and whistles, the nicknacks or trumpery stock of a tinker or packman.

tankards

Pint *stoups* hae lang lugs. Scott *Rob Roy* xxvi. *Drink leads to unguarded talk.*

Ye're as lang tunin your pipes as anither wad play a spring. (18th cent.)

tangled bobbin

A *ravelled pirn*, To wind, redd, etc. (16th cent.) *Of difficulties deliberately or unwittingly created.* See Intro. (Current)

nose

As plain as the *niz* on a man's face. (1706 and current) *Plain as a pikestaff.*

natural ... smell

It is *kindlie* that the *poke saur* o the herrin. (16th cent.) *Children take after their parents' foibles.*

peck

Pickle in your ain pock neuk. (a. 1628) Scott *Rob Roy* xxiii, *Heart of Midlothian* xxviii. *i.e. find the means from your own resources.*

bag-pudding

A *pock-puddin*. An 18th-century nickname in Scotland for an Englishman, from their supposed gluttony. Scott *Old Mortality* xxi. (Current)

putty

It winna *pottie*. (Current) *English: It won't wash.*

To talk like a prent buik. (Current) i.e. learnedly. Scott *lives of the Novelists* (1821): To use a Scottish phrase, to talk, etc.

To be the price of. (Current) *To serve one right.*

Ye're no sae puir as ye peep. (1721) *On pleading poverty.* (Current)

The wind aye blaws in the puir man's face. (Current) A Shetland proverb.

70

He's aye pittin on a puir mouth. (19th cent.) *Pleading poverty or misery*. A more modern version is, To hae on a sair face.

To mak one's *putt* guid. (19th cent.) *To gain one's object, carry one's point*. (Current) Cf. putt and row = *with patient persistent effort*.   *push, nudge*

A ragged *cowt* may pruive a guid geldin. (1736) For Burns's version see *A Dream* xi.   *colt*

It's rainin/*dingin* on puir men and pikestaves/auld wives and pipe stapples/Jeddart staves. (18th cent.) *To rain cats and dogs*.   *pelting*

To gar the key keep the castle and the rash *bus* keep the cow. (15th cent.) See Intro. *To maintain law and order*.   *bush*

Aye *reddin* the fire. (Current) *Always stirring up trouble*. To redd one's ain ribs is *to mind one's own business*.   *clear*

Muckle whistlin for little *redd* land/Mair whistlin than redd land. (18th cent.) English: *Much cry and little wool*. Cf. Lang on little yird.   *ploughed*

Redd aft, redd saft, Redd *seenil*, redd sair. A Moray version of the older Kame sindle, kame sair (*a*. 1600) *In correction it is better to be frequent and gentle than seldom and severe*.   *seldom*

The *redder* aye gets the reddin *straik*. Scott *Old Mortality* iv. (Current) Kelly (1721): He that meddles wi tulyies comes in for the reddin straik.   *Pacifier ... stroke or blow*

Red hand (With the). (15th cent.) A Scots legal expression=*with blood on one's hand, flagrante delicto, in the act.* Scott coined the form 'red-handed' (*Ivanhoe* xxv.)

Not to lat the reek blaw on. (*a.* 1500). *To coddle or cosset.* (Current)

It's a sour reek where the guidwife dings the guidman. (1721)

troublesome   A reeky house and a girnin wife will mak a man a *fashious life.* (1736)

clamorous wife   A house wi a reek and a *wife wi a raird* will mak a man rin to the door (1832) See Intro. for the above three.

That'll mak her ribbons reel. (Current) *That'll shake her.* A Moray saw.

He's no to ride the water on. (19th cent.) *i.e. is untrustworthy.* (Current)

He's as welcome as water in a riven ship. (1736)

He sits fu still that has a riven breek. (*a.* 1600) See Intro.

Rob Gibb's contract—stark love and kindness. (16th cent.) The answer of Rob Gibb, master of the horse to King James V, when asked why he served him. The expression later became a popular or loyal toast.

distaff   To hae ither tow on one's *rock.* (*a.* 1600) *To have other fish to fry.*

lose   Rowan tree and reid threid Mak the witches *tyne* their speed/Haud the witches aa in dreid. Red as the colour of fire was considered to be an effective deterrent to witchcraft.

pull nor tear   It'll neither *rug nor rive.* (Current in the North-east)
apart   Especially of very tough food.

Scots Saws

To get the ruit and the rise o't. (Current) *To be told
the whole story from the beginning.*

S

To be putten to aa the seats o the saiddle. (1825) *To be
driven to every shift.* A favourite saying of Scott.
"Obviously borrowed from the uneasy sensations of
one who feels his seat on horseback too hard for
him" (Jamieson's Dictionary).

He never rides the day he saiddles. (Current) *He never
keeps his promise.*

Weel *saipet* is half shaven. (*c.* 1800) Ascribed to Prin-
cipal Hill of St Andrews University as a translation
of Horace's *Dimidium facti qui coepit habet*, 'well
begun is half done'.   *soaped*

It's a sair dung bairn that daurna greet. (*a.* 1600) Also
in mediaeval English: Sore is he bett, that darre not
wepe.

He pits on his sair face. (Current) *i.e. looks abject to
elicit sympathy.*

Keep aye something for a sair fit/leg. (Current) *For a
rainy day.*

He will never send you awa wi a sair hert. (1721 and
still current) *He'll promise you anything.*

I'll gie you a *sarkfu* o sair banes. (1721) Scott *Guy
Mannering* xlv.   *shirtful*

He was wrappit in his mither's sark tail. (1721) See
Intro.

He'll never mak saut til his kail. (18th cent.) Make a
living. (Current)

Scots Saws

salve, ointment

Seek your *saw* whar ye got your sair. (1736) *Seek redress from the person who wronged you.* (Current)

Lat the saw sink to the sair. (Current) An excuse for medication by internal applications of whisky.

They have said; what say they; lat them say. (16th cent.) The motto of the Keiths of Inverurie in contempt of public opinion. Adopted by Marischal College, Aberdeen, founded by the Keiths.

I'm no a scone o that bakin. (Current) *Not one of that sort.* Originally the expression was: One scone of a baking is enough. Kelly: It is unreasonable to expect two gratuities out of one thing.

I wish you may have Scotch to carry you to bed. (1721) Kelly: Spoken when our companions, beginning to take with the drink, begin to speak Latin, believing that by and by they will be at that pass that they will be able to speak no language. No longer current; modern drunks seldom speak Latin.

A Scots convoy. (19th cent.) When a host sees his guest all or part of the way home. (Current) For 'A Kelso convoy' as a much more curt form of leave-taking, see Scott *Antiquary* xxx.

Ye hae a guid Scots tongue in your heid. (1721) *You can speak up for yourself.* Scott *Rob Roy* xxvi.

Scotsmen are aye wise ahint the hand. (16th cent.) *Wise after the event.* If not current it ought to be.

Scotsmen aye reckon frae an ill hour/take their mark from a mischief. (1721) *i.e. remember their disasters most.*

The Englishman weeps, the Irishman sleeps but the Scottishman gangs while he gets it. (1721) Kelly: A pretended account of the behaviour of these three nations, when they want meat. Things have changed nowadays.

74

Scots Saws

A Paisley/Glesca screwdriver. (Current) *A hammer.*
See Intro.

O wad some power the giftie gie us, To see oursels as
ithers see us. Burns *To a Louse* viii.

A seed in one's teeth. (18th cent.) English: *A flea in
one's ear.*

Ye shape shune by your ain *shauchled* feet. (1721)   *shambling*
Judge others by yourself.

Shame's past the *shed* o your hair. (16th cent.) Of a   *parting*
brazen-faced person.

He thinks himsel nae sheep-shank. (18th cent.) *No
small beer.* Cf. Burns *Epistle to J. Lapraik* xii,
Brigs o Ayr 5.

There was mair tint at Sherramuir, whar the
Hielandman lost his father and his mither and a
guid buff belt worth baith o them. (18th cent.)
Scott repeats the first clause frequently. The name
of the battle, Sherramuir, Flodden, Culloden, varies
according to the historical knowledge and sym-
pathies of the speaker, in the spirit of the above
saying about Scotsmen reckoning frae an ill hour.

To set out the brunt side o your shin. (18th cent.) *To
step out proudly, swagger.*

A *shored* tree stands lang in the wuid. (*a.* 1600)   *threatened*
Threatened folk live long.

Never to luik ower one's shouder. (Current) *Never to
look back, to progress steadily.*

Better wear out shune than sheets. (17th cent.) A
health aphorism.

As *sib* as sieve and riddle. (15th cent.) Dunbar   *related*
Testament of A. Kennedy 55.

It's guid to be sib to siller. (Current) Cf. Nae friend like the penny.

Siller sick. (15th cent.) *Greedy for money.* Henryson *Fox, Wolf and Cadger* 85.

To simmer and winter (about) a thing. (17th cent.) *To take a long time to think it over, to take a long close look at.* Common in Galt. (Current)

hurt

To hae baith the *skaith* and the scorn. (16th cent.) Montgomerie *Cherrie and Slae* xvi. Kelly: Spoken when one gets a hurt and another laughs at it.

Better twa skaiths than ae sorrow. (*a.* 1600) Kelly: Losses may be repaired but sorrow will break the heart.

He has a sliddery grip that has an eel by the tail. (1832) Especially those on the Thames.

Quha that surest dois keip him, sonest dois slyd. (*a.* 1500) *Against being cocksure.*

sling-stone

Like a *slung-stane.* (18th cent.) *Like a bolt from the blue.*

mare

'There's sma sorrow at our pairtin,' as the auld *mear* said to the broken cairt. (1721) Scott *Rob Roy* xxvii.

stumble

A horse may *snapper* on fower feet. (*a.* 1600) *The race is not always to the swift.*

Like sna aff a dyke. (Current) *Disappearing quickly, melting away.*

Sodger-cled but major-mindit. (20th cent.) *With aspirations above one's circumstances.* Possibly of Boer War vintage.

I wad hae something to look at on Sunday. (1721) Kelly: Spoken when we complain of one's wife or husband that they are not big, comely or sightly. Possibly still in mind but no longer in use.

Scots Saws

Better be *sonsie* as sune up. (1721) *Of one built for comfort rather than speed.*   *lucky*

A *yeld* sow was never guid to *grices*. (*a.* 1600) *Childless people don't care for the children of others.* (Current)   *barren ... young pigs*

As the soo fills the draff sours. (*a.* 1600) *The more one eats the less appetising it becomes.* (Current)

The souter gae the soo a kiss; 'Humph', quo she, 'It's for my *birse*'. (1721) Kelly: Of those whose service we suppose to be mercenary. Scott: From an ancient Scottish canzonetta.   *bristles*

Like a soo playin on a *trump*. (1721) Scott *Rob Roy* xxv. Of something ludicrously clumsy or ungainly.   *Jew's harp*

It's ill makin a silk purse frae a soo's lug (or a toutin horn frae a tod's tail). (*a.* 1700) (Current)

To keep a calm *souch*. (Current) *To hold one's tongue.* Scott *The Abbot* xvii.   *whisper*

To tak in the warld by speed o fit. (Current) *To be a hustler.*

Monie a ane speirs the road he kens fu weel. (*a.* 1600) *Of sly or diffident persons.*

There's naething in his heid but what the spune pits in (and the bane kame rugs out). (Current) *Stupidity in a nutshell.*

As tired as she had washen a spune. (*a.* 1568) Ironical.

I garred him stand yont. (18th cent. and current) *i.e. keep his distance.*

The stang/tongue o the trump. (1721) Scott *Guy Mannering* xxxii, *Bride of Lammermoor* xxv. The essential part or person in any activity. (Current)

sting	To *stang* like an adder. (15th cent.) Dunbar *Changes of Lyfe* 141.
stave ... drinking cup	A *stap* out o one's *bicker*. (18th cent.) *A cut in one's income or resources.*
	To step aside is human. Burns *Address to the Unco Guid* vii.
	Aa Stewarts are no sib to the King. (*a.* 1600) Kelly: Spoken when people boast of some great man of their name. A retort to name-droppers. (Current)
	To mak a stick to brak your ain back. (Current) Frequent in various forms *a.* 1600: He has brocht a staff to his awin heid; His awin wand beats him; Many gives a staff to brek their awin heid.
bullock	There's aye some water whar the *stirkie* drouns. (18th cent. and current) *No smoke without fire.*
	To be putten in the stirkie's sta. (Current) *To be displaced by a new brother or sister in the attentions of one's parents, to have one's eye put out.*
plaster statue	To stand like a *stoukie*. (19th cent.) *Like a poker, in a stiff sheepish manner.*
	Ye could hae bund me wi a strae. (1808) English: *knocked me down with a feather.*
	As weel sune as syne. (Current) Montgomerie *Sonnets* xx, Scott *Rob Roy* xviii. *The sooner the better.*
	They that get the word o sune risin may lie in their bed aa day. (1737) *On the value of reputation, deserved or not.*
	There was a wife that kept her supper for her breakfast and she was deid or day. (1721) An anecdotal proverb on excessive thrift.
	To sweep one's tails upon. (Current) *To treat with disdain, to 'cut'.*

Scots Saws

The swine's gane through it. (1721) Of a project
falling through. See Intro.

Ye breed o Kilpikc's/Sangster's/Saughton swine;
your *neb* is never out o an ill turn. (18th cent.) *snout*

T

Nae man has a *tack* o his life. (1736) In con- *lease*
tradistinction to the notion of a lease of life.
(Current)

He's in wi the tack. (Current) *Part and parcel of the
concern, inextricably involved in the business.*

Haud *Taggie* by the tail. (18th cent.) *Never give up* *tagtailed cow*
hold on what is secure: a bird in the hand ...

Tak your ain tale hame. Scott *Antiquary* xxvii. *Take
your advice to yourself.*

Ye can mak neither tap, tail nor *main* o't. (*a.* 1600) *the body of a*
Head nor tail. *story*

He *tarrows* early that tarrows on his kail. (*a.* 1600) *is surfeited*
Kelly: Spoken when men complain before they see
the utmost that they will get.

Never tak the tawse when a word will do the turn.
(1721)

Tak a lass wi the tear in her ee. Galt *Entail* III. xxviii,
Scott *Surgeon's Daughter* iv. In grief at the loss of a
fiancé or husband, 'on the rebound'.

What's in my *wame* is no in my testament. (1721) *belly*
Kelly: an excuse for eating rather than keeping
what is before us. *Carpe diem.*

That's a teed ba. (1736) *A success at the outset, cut
and dry from the start.* Scott *Redgauntlet* Let. xiii.

Nae man can tether time nor tide. Burns *Tam o Shanter* 7.

The thing that's dune the day is no to dae the morn. (Current) English: *One hour today is worth two tomorrow; no time like the present.*

There's my thoum/We'll weet thoums on that. (17th cent.) *Agreed, That's a bargain.* From the ancient practice of parties to a bargain licking their thumbs and pressing them together as a sign of agreement.

That's abune your thoum. (18th cent.) *Beyond your powers.*

To whistle on one's thoum. (18th cent.) Cf. Chaucer: To pipe in an ivy leaf. i.e. to hide one's mortification. Scott *Heart of Midlothian* xviii.

Keep your thoum on that. (16th cent.) *Keep that under your hat.* (Current)

He couldna bite his ain thoum. (Current) Of one very drunk.

twisted It's a *thrawn*-faced wean that's gotten against the father's will. (1721) Kelly: Kindness extorted comes always with a bad grace.

Every man's man had a man, and that made the Threave fa. (1721) On the dangers of delegating responsibility. Threave Castle, the stronghold of the Douglases in Kirkcudbrightshire, is said to have fallen to the attack of James II through the laxness of subordinates.

lost Tak tent o time ere time be *tint.* (16th cent.) A common proverb in most lands. The motto is often inscribed on sun-dials.

Tyne hert, tyne aa. (1721) Scott *Heart of Midlothian* 1. *Never say die.* (Current) For variants see next.

Scots Saws

Have you gear, have you nane, Tine hert and aa is gane. (1721) Scott *Heart of Midlothian* i. On a 17th-century mazer is the inscription: Tyne geir tyne little, Tyne honour tine muckle, Tyne hert tyne all.

Between the tynin and the winnin. (17th cent.) Originally a legal expression. Hoevering between success and failure. Scott *Redgauntlet* xx.

A tinkler ne'er was a town taker; A tailor was ne'er a hardy man; Nor yet a *wabster leal* o his trade; Nor ever were sin the warld began. (1832) These three trades were proverbially suspect in many countries.   *weaver honest*

It's no tint that a friend gets. (*a.* 1600) (Current)

It's ill tamin tod's *birds*/The tod's bairn's are ill to tame. (18th cent.) The disadvantages of a bad upbringing.   *cubs*

Wae's the wife that wants the tongue but weel's the man that gets her. (1832) Comment is superfluous.

Touch not the cat *but* a glove. The motto of Clan Macintosh, whose crest is the wild cat. Mind your manners when dealing with them.   *without*

A new tout on an auld horn. (16th cent.) *Old hat.* (Current)

To lat the tow gang wi the bucket. (Current) *To write off one's losses.*

He's the gear that winna *traik*. (1736) *A good solid dependable sort.*   *deteriorate*

Better a tume house than an ill tenant. (1721 and current) *On getting rid of wind.*

A tume purse maks a *blate* merchant. (*a.* 1600) Occasionally heard.   *bashful*

Twa to fecht and ane to *redd*. (Current) The ideal number of children in a family.   *settle*

U

unserved

Them that comes unbidden sits *unsaired*. (Current) Cf. Montgomerie *Cherrie and Slae* lxxviii. On gate-crashing.

Untimeous spurring spills the steid. Montgomerie *Cherrie and Slae* xxix.

If aa be guid that is upcome. (1644) *If all is as good as it looks*.

Wha daes the utmost that he can will whiles dae mair. Burns *To Dr Blacklock* viii.

He's worth nae weel that can bide nae wae. (1856) A Berwickshire proverb.

Walth gars wit waver. (*a.* 1600) Scott *St Ronan's Well* xv.

Lay your wame to your winnin. (1832) *Balance your budget*.

Lat his ain wand ding him. (*a.* 1600) *Let him stew in his own juice*.

Want is the warst o't. (1721) Kelly: When one must take a mean thing or want all. The choice of the devil or the deep sea.

It's a brave warld if it would last, and Heaven at the hinderend. (1727) *All this and Heaven too!* The modern version significantly leaves out the second part: It's a braw warld gin it lest.

Scots Saws

He's no sic a gowk as to *wise* the water by his ain mill. (1721)

We'll ne'er ken the worth o the water/Ye never miss the water till the wall gangs dry. (1721) Also quoted by Benjamin Franklin.

He's war to water than to corn. (1832) *Fonder of his drink than his food.*

Dip in your water afore ye wade it. (Current) *Proceed with caution.*

It's weak in the *waw*, like Barr's cat. (1835) Barr may have kept his cat on scrimp rations.

It's Wednesday through aa the warld. (*a.* 1779) Said to be an expression to ward off witchcraft.

Weel/Wise and warld-like. (Current) *Normal in health and appearance, especially of a new-born child.*

He's weel worth sorrow that buys it wi his ain siller. (1737) *He deserves all that is coming to him.*

After word comes *weird* (fair fa them that ca mo madam). (*a.* 1600) Kelly: A facetious answer to them who call you by a higher title than your present station deserves ... as if you would say, 'All in good time.'

Like wha but him. (1715) Said of a conceited self-assured person. Cf. 'Fair fa mysel' similarly used.

Monie think mair o wha says a thing than o what the thing is that's said. Scott *Rob Roy* xxvi.

There's a *whap* in the *raip*. (*a.* 1628) *There's a snag, something amiss.*

Ye'll get him whar ye left him. (Current) Said of one of an equable placid disposition.

direct

wail

one's fate

hitch ... rope

short sword ... Monie tynes the half-merk *whinger* for the halfpenny
strap *whang.* (*a.* 1600) English: *To spoil the ship (earlier sheep) for a hapenny worth of tar.*

To come through the whins. (Current) *To come through hardship.*

Freedom and whisky gang thegither. Burns *Earnest Cry and Prayer* Ps. vii.

Whisky: the Auld kirk, the blue, Donald Blue, the hard, the real Mackay, mountain dew, the stuff(ie), peat-reek.

He kens hoo to butter a whitin. (18th cent.) Of flattery: *how to lay it on thick.* A pun between whitin, flattery, and whitin, the fish.

gallows-rope The water will ne'er waur the *widdie.* (*a.* 1600) *One will never be drowned who is destined to be hanged.*

It's nae lauchin to girn in a widdie. (1736)

An ill wife and a new-kindlit candle sud aye hae their heids hauden doun. (1736)

want He has *faut* o a wife that mairries mam's pet. (1736)

Nae man can thrive unless his wife will lat him. (1736)

Ye may drive the deil into a wife but ye'll ne'er ding him out o her. (1736)

rest The deith o his first wife made sic a hole in his hert that aa the *lave* slippit through. (*a.* 1600)

Ye never died o winter yet. (Current) *You'll survive all your difficulties.*

I've seen wiser eatin girse. (Current) Of a stupid person.

To get the *wissel* o your groat/*plack*. (18th cent.) *change . . .*
Burns *Epistle to J. Rankin* ix. *To be paid out in* *farthing*
one's own coin.

His wame thinks his *wizzen*'s cut. (Current) Of *gullet*
someone desperately hungry.

Sen word is thrall and thocht is only free. Ascribed to
King James I (*a.* 1437).

Ye'll dae onything but work and rin eirands. (19th
cent.) On laziness.

Ance *wuid* and ay the waur. (16th cent.) *i.e. getting* *mad*
madder and madder, incurably daft.

As fu's a wulk. (19th cent.) One of many similes for
'drunk'. (Current)

Yule is young on Yule even (24 Dec.) and auld in St
Stephen (26 Dec.) (1721) Kelly: Spoken when
people are much taken with novelties and as soon
weary of them.

The bag to the auld *stent* and the belt to the Yule bore. *stretch*
(1721) Kelly: Meaning that we eat as heartily as we
did at Christmas.

I'll bring your Yule belt to the Beltane bore. (1721)
The bore being the hole in the belt to which the
buckle is adjusted, expanded at Christmas and con-
tracted at Mayday when the winter store is running
low.

Informal expressions of greeting, good wishes, etc.

Nowadays such expressions are mainly stereotyped repetitions of the standard English form but Scots had its own set of these in former times and some of these have survived, especially in the speech of older folk to this day. The Scots think of themselves as affable and friendly people, quite unlike the epithet 'dour' applied to them by their southern neighbours, and as effusive in welcoming friend and stranger alike. To be on terms of "Fair guid een and fair guid day" in fact indicates nothing more than formal civility and a certain reserve or distance in one's manner. Someone on a friendly call would have expected a warm "Seil o (Blessings on) your face" or "Fair fa your honest hert" or Weel's me (Happy am I) on the sicht o you", for today's "How nice to see you again", and it is these that Burns conflated in addressing the haggis, "Fair fa your honest sonsie face". Carlyle gives as 'an expressive Annandale phrase of the completest welcome' the words "Ye hae will and waygate", as much as to say, "Come in and make yourself at home.' The usual greeting "How do you do?" or "How are you?" has different idiomatic renderings in different dialects. "Hou's aa wi you?" is fairly general. "Hou dae ye fend?" in the South-west, "What fettle?" and "Hou're ee lestin?" in the Borders and "Fat like?" in the North-east. To which the answer, depending on the circumstances, might be, "Brawly, thank ye", or "No bad considerin", or "I canna compleen", or the more old-fashioned formulae, "Livin and life-thinkin", or "The better ye dae weel", or "Aa the better for you speirin; speir ower again", or, ironically, "Herthale and sillerless; a hunder pound wad dae me nae hairm", or the philosophical answer of the very stout old lady, "Juist sic and sae; there's ower muckle o me to be aa weel at ae time". The guest who made a show of being in a hurry and unwilling to take a seat would be urged to do so with the words, "It's as cheap sittin as standin." And the invitation "Won't you join us?" would be expressed as "Come into the body o the kirk".

Certain formulae were reserved for special occasions, as "Grace and growin to the bairn" at a christening, "Happy feet" to a newly-married couple, it being of vital importance whether the visitors to their new home had 'lucky' or 'unlucky' feet. To anyone in a new house or at the new year the wish was "Lang may your lum reek" or a more expansive verse might be recited like this one:

> "May the best ye've ever seen be the warst ye'll ever see,
> May the mouse ne'er leave your girnel wi the tear-drap in
> its ee,
> May ye aye keep hale and hertie till ye're auld eneuch to
> die,
> May ye aye be juist as happy as I wish ye aye to be."

An expression of goodwill would be answered by "Sae fa you" i.e. "the same to you"; and the parting guest would be sped on his way by the jocular "Be guid and ye'll be bonnie" and the warm invitation "Haste ye back"; and the guest would respond with the old wish "Guid nicht and joy be wi you aa", which grew into a song in the 18th century and remained as the song of parting till it was replaced by Burns's *Auld Lang Syne*.

English Sayings and their Scots equivalents

As has already been said, the same proverb or proverbial phrase may be rendered in Scots through a different metaphor or simile from that in English or in a different form of words, which may be grammatical or conceptual or lexical and which for want of a better term may be called an idiom. It is in fact in idiom that much of the distinctiveness of Scots speech lies and a short selection of such is given below. Others may be found in the main list of proverbs above. For a full repertoire the pages of *The Dictionary of the Older Scottish Tongue* and *The Scottish National Dictionary* should be consulted. It is of course to be noted that as in the case of all idiomatic differences between languages the equivalence in meaning may not be exact and that one idiom may have connotations absent from the other. Much interest and insight may be derived from studying such subtleties and refinements in the distinctions.

It was his Achilles' heel.   It was a hair in his neck.

Take your advice to yourself.   Tak your ain tale hame.

To upset the apple-cart.   To cowp the kirn/creels/cran.

To be still around (alive).   To be aye to the fore.

He has arrived, made the grade.   His breid's baken. He may set by the girdle.

The average man, the hoi polloi.   The common five-echts.

To bark up the wrong tree.   To be up the wrang close.

Never to bat an eye.   Never to jee one's ginger.

He knows how many beans make five.   He kens the load frae the croun o the causey.

He thinks himself no small beer.   He thinks himsel nae sheep-shank.

I'll bet, I'll be bound.   I'se warrant.

To kill two birds with one stone.   To fell twa dogs wi ae bane.

To be blind to one's faults.   No to see daylicht til.

Like a bolt from the blue.   Like a slung-stane.

To balance gains and losses.   To lay the heid o the soo to the tail o the grice.

The business just broke even.   The business juist washed its face.

You can't eat your cake and have it.   It's ill bringin but what's no ben.

Like a cat on hot bricks.   Like a hen on a het girdle.

To stand on ceremony.   To stand upon stappin-stanes.

Charity begins at home.   Keep your ain fish-guts to your ain sea-maws.

To get it off your chest.   To redd your crap.

Go and chase yourself.   Gang and whistle on your thoum.

Counting your chickens before they are hatched.   Caukin the claith afore the wab be in the lume.   Cuttin afore the point.

To carry coals to Newcastle.   To cairry saut to Dysart.

To be paid in one's own coin.   To get the wissel o your groat.

Scots Saws

When the crunch comes. When hard comes to hard. When it comes to the bit.

As clear as crystal. As plain as parritch.

It's all cut and dry/ It's all sewn up. It's a teed ba.

That cut him down to size/ That shut him up. That pat the branks on him.

A past master at (his trade). A deacon at (his craft).

To keep one's distance. To stand yont.

He would talk the hind legs off a donkey. He has a tongue that wad clip clouts.

Down the drain. Doun the stank.

I'll be even with you. I'll see day about wi you.

To play fast and loose. To play Jock Needle Jock Preen.

The fat's in the fire. The deil's gane ower Jock Webster.

You could have knocked me down with a feather. Ye could hae bund me wi a strae.

They are all birds of a feather. They are aa ae oo.

To burn one's fingers. To scaud one's mou (in ither folks' kail).

All is fish that comes to his net. He has a crap for aa corn.

To have other fish to fry. To hae ither tow on one's rock.

I sent him away with a flea in his ear. I sent him awa wi a seed in his teeth.

A game chicken. A great warrior/A bonnie fechter.

To be led up the garden path/taken for a ride. To be taen to the fair.

That shut him up. That liddet his mull/That pat his gas at a peep.

People who live in glasshouses should not throw stones. He sud hae a hale pow that cas his neibour nittie now.

To be still going strong. To be livin and lifelike.

To grease one's palm. To glack one's mittens.

Let's shake hands on it. There's my thoum on that.

To have one's hands full. To hae one's ain adae.

As well be hanged for a sheep as a lamb/ In for a penny in for a pound. Ne'er gang to the deil wi a dishclout on your heid.

Keep that under your hat. Keep your thoum on that.

Old hat. A new tout on an auld horn.

I could make neither head nor tail of it. There was neither tap, tail nor main til't.

Heaven helps those that help themselves. Tak help at your elbows.

To show a clean pair of heels. To mak your feet your friend.

To throw the helve after the hatchet. To lat the tow gang wi the bucket.

Honesty is the best policy. Out the hiegate is aye fair play.

Scots Saws

Hurrah for England!   Scotland yet!

To be a hustler/pusher.   To tak in the warld by speed o fit.

To judge others by yourself.   Ye shape shune by your ain shauchled
feet.

Let him stew in his own juice.   Lat his ain wand ding him.

To jump for joy.   To dance one's lane.

It's a long lane that has no turning.   It's bare muir that ye gang
throu and no find a heather cow.

To lead on/ up the garden path.   To draw a strae afore.

You are taking your life in your hands.   There's fey bluid in your
heid.

The life and soul of the affair.   The stang o the trump.

To be at loggerheads.   To be at the knag and the widdie.

He's too long in the tooth for that.   There's ower monie nicks in his
horn.

Better half a loaf than no bread.   Better half egg than tume dowp.

He never looked back.   He never luikit ower his shoulder.

Hang first and try afterwards/ Lydford law.   Jeddart justice.

To make or mar.   To mak a kirk or a mill o't.

To take the mickey out of.   To tak the nap aff.

To put the miller's eye out.   To droun the miller.

Not in the mood/ Out of humour.   Aff the fang.

Much in little.   Guid gear in sma bouk.

To keep mum.   To sing dumb/keep a calm souch/haud one's
whisht.

To put one's nose out of joint.   To pit out one's ee.

To get one's own back.   To get amends o.

He is a past-master at (his trade).   He's a deacon at (his craft).

To rob Peter to pay Paul.   To rive the kirk to theek the quier.

To have a rod in pickle for.   To lay something in saut for/ To saut
somebody's kail/brose.

Any port in a storm.   Better a wee bus than nae bield.

To keep the pot boiling.   To haud the cuddie reekin.

He's not the clean potato.   He's no the berry (nor yet the bus it
grew on).

There's no time like the present.   The thing that's dune is no to dae.

To swallow one's pride.   To tak the bit and the buffet.

It never rains but it pours.   Ill comes upon waur's back.

To keep something for a rainy day.   To keep something for a sair
fit/leg.

On the rebound (in a broken love affair).   Wi the tear in her ee.

To make a red-letter day of something.   To strik a hack in the
cruik/post.

90

Scots Saws

To be rooted to the spot. To stand like a stoukie.
To have second thoughts. To tak the rue.
It serves him right. It's the price o him/It's weel wared on him.
To fight with one's shadow. To fecht wi one's ain taes/wi the wind.
He'll never fill his father's shoes. He winna rive his father's
  bonnet.
Always talking shop. Cadgers are aye crackin o cruik saiddles.
To be on short commons. To get a dish o whummle.
There's a skeleton in every cupboard. There's a dub at ilka door.
To sit on the sidelines. Neither to dance nor haud the candle.
To crack a nut with a sledge-hammer. Never tak a forehammer to
  brak an egg (when ye can dae it wi a penknife).
Small is beautiful. Mickledom is nae virtue.
You'll never smell that. That will never craw in your crap.
There is no smoke without fire. There's aye some water whaur the
  stirkie drouns.
There's a snag. There's a whap in the raip.
The sooner the better. As weel sune as syne.
To look very sorry for oneself. To pit on one's sair face.
It's no use crying over spilt milk. It's like butter in the black dog's
  hause.
It is too late to lock the stable door after the steed has been
  stolen. It's past joukin when the heid's aff.
At a standstill. Like a set mill.
To stick to one's story. To be at ae word.
A stuffed shirt. A tulchan.
A success from the start. A teed ba/ A peeled egg.
To be on tenterhooks. To be on hecklepins/ like a hen on a het
  girdle.
To set the Thames on fire. To set the heather on fire.
As bold as brass. Like wha but him.
To do one's thing. To ca one's gird.
Threatened folk live long. A shored tree stands lang.
To change one's tune. To tak one's word again.
Walls have ears. There's a drap in the house/ It's drappin suit.
It won't wash. It winna pottie.
I'll give you what for. I'll gie you your fairin/ I'll gar ye claw
  whar it's no yeukie.
To have the whiphand. To hae the heft and the blade in one's ain
  hand.
He is his mother's white-haired boy. His mither canna see daylicht
  til him.
As easy as winking. As easy as kiss-my-luif.

Scots Saws

Your wits are wool-gathering.   Your mind's aye chasin mice.
Much cry for little wool.   Muckle whistlin for little redd land.
A bad workman always blames his tools.   An ill shearer ne'er got a
  guid heuk.
The world's a small place.   They gang far about that dinna meet ae
  day.